LONDON'S EAST END

FAMILY HISTORY FROM PEN & SWORD

The Family History Web Directory	*Jonathan Scott*
Tracing British Battalions on the Somme	*Ray Westlake*
Tracing Great War Ancestors	*BHTV*
Tracing History Through Title Deeds	*Nat Alcock*
Tracing Secret Service Ancestors	*Phil Tomaselli*
Tracing the Rifle Volunteers	*Ray Westlake*
Tracing Your Air Force Ancestors	*Phil Tomaselli*
Tracing Your Ancestors	*Simon Fowler*
Tracing Your Ancestors from 1066 to 1837	*Jonathan Oates*
Tracing Your Ancestors Through Letters and Personal Writings	*Ruth A Symes*
Tracing Your Aristocratic Ancestors	*Anthony Adolph*
Tracing Your Army Ancestors	*Simon Fowler*
Tracing Your Army Ancestors - 3rd Edition	*Simon Fowler*
Tracing Your Birmingham Ancestors	*Michael Sharpe, Michael Sharpe*
Tracing Your Black Country Ancestors	*Michael Pearson*
Tracing Your Boer War Ancestors	*Jane Marchese Robinson*
Tracing Your Canal Ancestors	*Sue Wilkes*
Tracing Your Channel Islands Ancestors	*Marie-Louise Backhurst*
Tracing Your Criminal Ancestors	*Stephen Wade*
Tracing Your East Anglian Ancestors	*Gill Blanchard*
Tracing Your East End Ancestors	*Jane Cox*
Tracing Your First World War Ancestors	*Simon Fowler*
Tracing Your Georgian Ancestors 1714–1837	*John Wintrip*
Tracing Your Glasgow Ancestors	*Ian Maxwell*
Tracing Your Great War Ancestors: The Gallipoli Campaign	*Simon Fowler*
Tracing Your Great War Ancestors: The Somme	*Simon Fowler*

Family History From Pen & Sword

Tracing Your Great War Ancestors: Ypres — Simon Fowler

Tracing Your Huguenot Ancestors — Kathy Chater

Tracing Your Jewish Ancestors — Rosemary Wenzerul

Tracing Your Jewish Ancestors - Second Edition — Rosemary Wenzerul

Tracing Your Labour Movement Ancestors — Mark Crail

Tracing Your Legal Ancestors — Stephen Wade

Tracing Your Liverpool Ancestors — Mike Royden

Tracing Your Liverpool Ancestors - Second Edition — Mike Royden

Tracing Your London Ancestors — Jonathan Oates

Tracing Your Medical Ancestors — Michelle Higgs

Tracing Your Merchant Navy Ancestors — Simon Wills

Tracing Your Northern Ancestors — Keith Gregson

Tracing Your Northern Irish Ancestors — Ian Maxwell

Tracing Your Northern Irish Ancestors - Second Edition — Ian Maxwell

Tracing Your Pauper Ancestors — Robert Burlison

Tracing Your Police Ancestors — Stephen Wade

Tracing Your Pre-Victorian Ancestors — John Wintrip

Tracing Your Prisoner of War Ancestors: The First World War — Sarah Paterson

Tracing Your Railway Ancestors — Di Drummond

Tracing Your Royal Marine Ancestors — Richard Brooks, Matthew Little

Tracing Your Rural Ancestors — Jonathan Brown

Tracing Your Scottish Ancestors — Ian Maxwell

Tracing Your Second World War Ancestors — Phil Tomaselli

Tracing Your Servant Ancestors — Michelle Higgs

Tracing Your Service Women Ancestors — Mary Ingham

Tracing Your Shipbuilding Ancestors — Anthony Burton

Tracing Your Tank Ancestors — Janice Tait, David Fletcher

Tracing Your Textile Ancestors — Vivien Teasdale

Tracing Your Twentieth-Century Ancestors — Karen Bali

Tracing Your Welsh Ancestors — Beryl Evans

Tracing Your West Country Ancestors — Kirsty Gray

Tracing Your Yorkshire Ancestors — Rachel Bellerby

Writing Your Family History — Gill Blanchard

Your Irish Ancestors — Ian Maxwell

LONDON'S EAST END

A Guide for Family and Local Historians

Jonathan Oates

First published in Great Britain in 2018 by
Pen & Sword Family History
an imprint of
Pen & Sword Books Ltd
47 Church Street
Barnsley
South Yorkshire
S70 2AS

Copyright (c) Jonathan Oates 2018

ISBN 978 1 52672 411 3

The right of Jonathan Oates to be identified as the Author of this Work has been asserted by him in accordance with the Copyright, Designs and Patents Act 1988.

A CIP catalogue record for this book is available from the British Library

All rights reserved. No part of this book may be reproduced or transmitted in any form or by any means, electronic or mechanical including photocopying, recording or by any information storage and retrieval system, without permission from the Publisher in writing.

Typeset in Ehrhardt MT by SRJ Info Jnana System Pvt Ltd.

Printed and bound by
CPI UK

Pen & Sword Books Ltd incorporates the imprints of Pen & Sword Archaeology, Atlas, Aviation, Battleground, Discovery, Family History, History, Maritime, Military, Naval, Politics, Railways, Select, Social History, Transport, True Crime, and Claymore Press, Frontline Books, Leo Cooper, Praetorian Press, Remember When, Seaforth Publishing and Wharncliffe.

For a complete list of Pen & Sword titles please contact
PEN & SWORD BOOKS LIMITED
47 Church Street, Barnsley, South Yorkshire, S70 2AS, England
E-mail: enquiries@pen-and-sword.co.uk
Website: www.pen-and-sword.co.uk

CONTENTS

Acknowledgements		vi
Introduction		1
1	What is the East End?	5
2	Working Lives in the East End	19
3	East End Poverty and Attempts at its Relief	37
4	Crime and Vice	53
5	War and Riot	69
6	Religions in the East End	85
7	Moving in – and out of – the East End	109
8	Leisure Activities	119
9	Schooling and Health	129
10	General Sources	145
11	Places to See and Visit	161
Conclusion		177
Bibliography		179
Index		183

ACKNOWLEDGEMENTS

John Coulter, Paul Howard Lang and Lindsay Siviter, have, as always, been very generous with the loan of pictures to use in this book. In addition, Lindsay has lent books and maps to help with the book's content. Several people have read the book's text to point out any errors and omissions, these being Malcolm Barr-Hamilton, archivist at Tower Hamlets Archives, and two family historians, Caroline Lang and John Gauss; however any remaining ones are the author's sole responsibility. I would also like to extend my thanks to the staff at Tower Hamlets Archives and at the London Metropolitan Archives for having provided numerous documents and other material which have been used to illustrate the text of this book.

This book is dedicated to Malcolm and the team at Tower Hamlets Local History Library & Archives.

INTRODUCTION

In the popular mind and in the media, the East End conjures up a number of images. First, since 1985 there has been the television soap opera, *East Enders*, set in the contemporary East End, and in more recent years, the highly popular Sunday night viewing, *Call the Midwife*, which was set in Poplar and was initially based on the memoirs of a midwife who worked there from the 1950s. Secondly there is crime, whether it is the alleged glamour of the Kray gangsters of the 1960s or the horror and the mystery of the Whitechapel serial killer of 1888, known only as Jack the Ripper. Others may recall the Blitz which had an undue impact on the East End and in which the defiant spirit of London was shown at its authentic best. Political historians will recall the 'Battle of Cable Street' of 1936 where the police fought with anti-Fascists. There is also the repute of the East End as being where the worst scenes of nineteenth-century poverty were experienced. The East End is thus known as an entity more than most other parts of London.

The East End is rather more than the sum of these 'highlights', although these are all part of its story and its identity. The East End is not identical to East London as designated by postcodes or geography. In fact the term itself was not employed until the nineteenth century and was in common usage by the early twentieth century. It refers to those districts which make up the post-1965 London Borough of Tower Hamlets and, it can be argued, the former borough of Shoreditch which is to its immediate north and now part of the London Borough of Hackney. This is a district which lies to the east of Bishopsgate, to the north of the River Thames and as far east as the border of what was once the county of Middlesex (Greater London continues to the east, into part of Essex, to districts such as East and West Ham, now the London Borough of Newham).

It is important to remember that the East End is not a homogeneous entity, but, as with London itself, a collection of a number of settlements which have expanded, both in terms of population and buildings, over time. Some border the Thames, such as Limehouse, Wapping and the Isle of Dogs, so have a different character to the more inland parishes such as Spitalfields and Shoreditch.

This book is an attempt to examine the sources of information that exist for a study of the East End, whether it be a family history search or a local history survey. The two branches of research are often seen as being far removed from each other, but they have more in common than is often realised. The former should be more than a hunt restricted to certain names but should consider the surroundings in which one's ancestors lived, worshipped, worked, played and died in order to put their lives in context. And local history is concerned with people, for without people there can be no history.

This book will survey sources which can shed a light on readers' East End ancestors and on the district's history. It will also discuss how information can be found out about the context of their lives by surveying the sources for the local history of the East End. Some of these sources can be found online, but much cannot and therefore visits to a number of record offices and libraries will be necessary to fully exploit all the material which awaits the researcher.

From the mid-nineteenth century to the mid-twentieth, the East End was one of the most densely populated parts of London. In the 1920s, two-thirds of a million people lived there. This was in part because of its poverty as families lived often in one or two rooms, compared to the, generally, more spacious accommodation of much of west and north London. It is likely that those with London ancestors will probably have some ancestors who lived in the East End, therefore.

It is assumed that the reader interested in family history will have some information to hand before they begin their quest; any facts or leads (because all verbal 'facts' should be checked if possible) from relatives; as well as civil registration certificates of births, marriages and deaths (from 1837 onwards; indexes available on Ancestry.co.uk and then can be ordered at www.gro.gov.uk) and the census returns for 1841–1911 (searchable on Ancestry.co.uk and other sites). Possession of these will provide a solid foundation for future research for these are the building

Introduction

Royal visit to Whitechapel, 1887 (collection of Lindsay Siviter).

blocks establishing who your nineteenth- and twentieth-century ancestors were, where they lived, where they were born and where they died, and their occupations and relationships to one another. Likewise, the local historian should have a general grasp of national and London history to begin with as this will provide a framework for a local study about poverty, politics or leisure or whatever is of interest.

The book is divided into eleven chapters. First there is a general introductory history of the East End. Chapter 2 discusses working lives and chapter 3, poverty and its relief by public and private means. Chapter 4 focuses on the sources for a study of criminals and their victims in the East End. We then turn to the East End's finest and grimmest hour during the world wars in chapter 5. Religions have played a significant part in the history of the local communities and this chapter examines the evidence of their impact. East End society has been diverse for centuries and the next chapter looks at how it is possible to ascertain information about the district's newcomers and equally important about those leaving it. Chapter 8 investigates sources which tell of how the inhabitants spent their hard-earned leisure hours. In chapter 9 schools, health and hospitals are explored. Then there is a general chapter about other useful sources for the locality's history and for family history not mentioned elsewhere. Finally, we will look at the places that a researcher should endeavour to visit in their work. There is also a bibliography with a selection of books for useful further reading.

The author has worked in archives in London since 1994 and has written four books already as guides to family history, ten books about London crime and criminals and seven books about London's local history. On his wife's side of his family, he has a number of Bignell ancestors who resided in nineteenth-century Shoreditch and were married at St Leonard's parish church.

Chapter 1

WHAT IS THE EAST END?

We need to briefly examine the East End's history in order to inform ourselves of the background to the material that is to be discussed in later chapters. As has already been made clear, it was not a homogeneous entity, but a number of distinct settlements which grew over time.

Origins and Medieval East End

Although there were some Roman settlements to the east of the City of London, the first fixed settlements of any size emerged after the Romans had left. The largest district was Stepney, which stretched from the eastern fringes of the City to the River Lea and from Mile End in the north to the Thames in the south, and takes its name from Stebunheath or Stebba's landing. Central was St Dunstan's church. This was the ancient manor, held by the bishop of London, a Saxon settlement, which was recorded in some detail in the Domesday Book of 1086. The population then stood at about 900 people, who worked on the land – arable, pasture, meadowland and woodland. There were also mills there. Hoxton was another East End Domesday manor.

One of the hamlets of the parish of Stepney was Bethnal Green, possibly of Saxon origin as Blithehale. Another was Whitechapel, named because there was a chapel there that was white. This began its existence as a medieval suburb of the City of London, on the main road to Essex.

To the east of Spitalfields, a mile along the main road, was, appropriately enough, Mile End. In this period it was dominated by the parish church of St Dunstan, surrounded by several large houses of the gentry. There were smaller clusters of housing around the manorial common land, where in 1381 Wat Tyler's rebels massed before marching on London. A few days later there was the fatal encounter between Richard II and the peasant rebel, in which the Lord Mayor killed the latter and the young King then effectively ended the rebellion.

Bow (once called Stratford Bow) and Bromley (not to be confused with the place of the same name to the south of Lewisham and in the county of Kent until 1965) were to the east, both with crossings of the Lea as the road ran from London to Colchester. Bromley grew up around a medieval nunnery. The first stone bridge in England was built here in the early twelfth century because Henry I's queen nearly drowned when crossing the ford. To the west of these was Bethnal Green. To the south were a number of hamlets on the north side of the Thames: Wapping, Ratcliff, Shadwell, Limehouse and Poplar, linked by the road named the High Way (so called because it was on higher ground than the riverside marshes).

Wapping, named after the Saxon Waeppa, was established as a settlement in the fourteenth century when the marshland had been reclaimed and water defences were built. Wharves then spread along the waterfront. Buildings had sprung up from the City to this district by the fifteenth century.

Limehouse was another small medieval Thameside settlement, which is known to have existed since the fourteenth century, though was initially known as Limekiln. This was naturally because of the lime kilns here when chalk was brought from Kent to be used in the London building business.

In the Middle Ages there were two major religious foundations in this part of London; the Cistercian priory of St Mary Graces, near the Tower of London, and St Mary Spital (from which the district Spitalfields takes its name). There was also the Royal Foundation of St Katharine's, also known as the Priory of St Leonard's in Bromley.

Hoxton and Haggerston were both mentioned in the Domesday Book and made up part of the manor of Shoreditch. The latter was at the junction of two old Roman roads but was not mentioned as an entity until 1148. As with neighbouring districts, there was a religious foundation, the Augustinian Priory of Holywell, which was also the major landowner here until the dissolution in 1539.

High Street, Whitechapel (collection of Lindsay Siviter).

All these places were quite distinct from another, with a great deal of open land between them – unlike the built-up area that was the cities of Westminster and London to the west. In the twelfth century Hoxton was described thus: 'the fields for pasture and open meadows, very pleasant, into which the river waters do flow and mills are tarried about with a delightful noise. Next lieth a great forest, in which are woody places for game'.

Early Modern East End

This period saw what was once a collection of hamlets surrounded by fields and pasture begin to be transformed. The hamlets became small towns and London began to spread eastwards. Yet they were still desirable places to live in. The medieval hamlets expanded considerably in these centuries. By about 1700 there were about 3,000 houses in Whitechapel, including many Jewish immigrants. Limehouse's population rose from about 2,000 in 1610 to 7,000 in 1710. Change, however, was variable as population growth in these districts was quite uneven.

These places were ruled by parishes and overseen, as was the whole of London (excepting the City) and Middlesex, by the Middlesex Quarter Sessions, a body of justices of the peace who dealt with disputes between the parishes and administrative matters as well as law and order. Growth occurred as the hamlets expanded in size. Stepney was no longer the principal body of local government as it had been in the Middle Ages when it had been the manor. Its size meant that it was too unwieldy a unit for administrative purposes. Instead its constituent parts formed their own self-governing parishes in the seventeenth and eighteenth centuries. These were Shadwell (1669), St George's in the East (1727), Spitalfields (1729), Bow and Limehouse (1730) and Bethnal Green (1743).

One reason for this growth was that industries and trade grew up along the Thames, as part of a national expansion of overseas commerce. Coal from Newcastle and goods from elsewhere in Britain were transported up the Thames. Malt and grain were shipped down the River Lea from Hertfordshire. Mills and bakeries sprang up at Bow, though some had existed there since the eleventh century.

There were still many farms in the district even by the eighteenth century. In Bromley there were 60 acres of market gardens as well as arable and pasture land. In Bethnal Green there was even more land employed for agriculture: 190 acres of arable land, 160 acres of grassland and 140 acres of market gardens. Some of this produce was sold and eaten locally and the rest was sold in the London markets. There were also brickfields in Bethnal Green providing material for building houses locally and in London.

Some parts were quite prosperous, such as Mile End, which until the early nineteenth century was a select place for merchants and gentry. Spitalfields flourished as a centre of the silk trade, which, from the seventeenth century, was dominated by the Huguenots, strengthening an industry which was already in existence. It was a fashionable address and was convenient for businessmen working in the City. Other merchants made their homes here, including German sugar refiners in Whitechapel and Baltic timber merchants in St George's parish. Handsome Georgian houses illustrated the prosperity of many residents in this district. Bethnal Green was once home to courtiers resident in mansions. However, Poplar was never attractive for the well to do. There were also theatres, new churches and from 1750, the London Hospital.

Shoreditch had a central role to play in London's theatrical history. James Burbage founded the first theatre in England here. It was there from 1576 to 1592 before moving to Southwark where it was re-erected and named The Globe. There was another local theatre, in 1577, titled

The Curtain, owned by one Henry Lanman in 1582. It existed here until 1625. Many actors lived in the vicinity and several were buried at the parish church.

The eighteenth century saw Britain's overseas trade grow spectacularly and London became a central market for luxury goods. Because of this, shipyards and docks were established here by the major trading companies, such as the East India Company. Ropeworks and other maritime industries emerged along the waterfronts to cater to the shipping that docked on the Thames. Cable Street was so called because of the many rope yards in the St George's district.

There was further industrial expansion in the following century. Enclosed docks made the place less confused. Secure storage was created to house bulky commodities such as sugar, tea and tobacco. Industry spread along the Lea and giant breweries at Spitalfields and Mile End were major employers of local labour. There were many small businesses, too, mostly in the clothing trade which had replaced the silk industry of the previous centuries. Much of this work was done in the home and employed many of the poor Jewish immigrants from Eastern Europe who arrived in the later nineteenth century, especially to Whitechapel, Spitalfields and Bethnal Green.

Limehouse (collection of John Coulter).

Many skilled artisans and craftsmen lived in St George's, alongside market gardeners scattered among patches of housing and common land. Maritime suppliers dominated Wapping, as John Stow remarked about Wapping High Street with 'alleys of small tenements and cottages, inhabited by sailors' victuallers'. There were also homes of the prosperous shipbuilders here, at least until the eighteenth century.

Shadwell and Ratcliff, two of the hitherto tiny riverside communities, grew considerably in this period. By 1669, Shadwell had about 8,000 residents, many of whom were mariners. Ratcliff had about 3,500 people in this century. Most were employed in various industries such as glassmaking and others more obviously related to maritime matters.

Jews and the Irish began to settle in this district. One of Cromwell's few pieces of liberal legislation was to allow the former to reside in England again (having been expelled from the country in the thirteenth century). A Jewish cemetery was established in Mile End in 1657. Danes and Swedes lived in St George's in the East by the eighteenth century.

Poverty existed, though nothing on the scale that was to be reached in the nineteenth century. John Stow, in the sixteenth century, wrote thus of Mile End, 'this common field, being sometime the beauty of the City on that part is so encroached upon by building of filthy cottages'. Of Whitechapel High Street he wrote that it was 'no small blemish on so famous a city'. John Wesley wrote in 1771, 'I began visiting those of our society who lived in Bethnal Green. Many of those I found in such poverty as few can conceive without seeing it'. Schools, almshouses and other institutions began to be erected in these parishes for the less well off. One of the first Nonconformist schools in the country was established in Hoxton in the later seventeenth century. Two almshouses were built in Bromley by 1613. In 1792 a Universal Medical Institute was in existence in St George's to provide free medicine and medical advice, being funded by private donations.

The reverberations of national history were also felt here. In 1556, 13 heretics were burnt at Bow as part of Queen Mary's campaign against Protestantism. Fortifications were built at Shadwell and Whitechapel to ward off any attack on London as Parliament defied Charles I when the civil war began in 1642.

The Nineteenth Century

It was in this century that the term 'the East End' was first coined. It was increasingly viewed by outsiders, often prosperous Londoners in the West End of London, as a centre of barbarism, poverty and vice. The hideous murders committed there in 1888 were held up as proof of this, but equally well-heeled reformers pointed out that this was a sign that reform – in health, housing and education – was vital. All agreed, though, that the East End was desperately poor. This was in contrast to the situation in previous centuries.

Social reformer Henry Mayhew wrote of Whitechapel, 'The poverty of these workers compels them to lodge wherever the rent of the rooms is lowest'. Later in the century Charles Booth referred to 'the eldorado of the East, a gathering together of poor fortune seekers; its streets full of buying and selling, the poor live on the poor'. According to him, in 1889, 45 per cent of the population lived below the subsistence level. The rector of Limehouse wrote in 1861, 'the parishioners are for the most part poor … There's an increase of low lodging houses for sailors ... and the removal of the more respectable families to other districts'. Apparently Shoreditch 'ranks second among eastern area boroughs in the percentage of persons living in poverty' because of the overcrowding and poverty in Hoxton.

By this time, the distinct villages that had made up the East End up to the eighteenth century had disappeared. In 1801 population had been about 142,000 and a century later it was almost 600,000. Furthermore, Shoreditch's population rose from 35,000 in 1801 to 129,000 in 1861, though it had undergone a slight decline to 117,706 in 1901. The district was a continuous urban sprawl of small streets, interspaced by roads, railways and canals (the Limehouse Canal, opened in 1770, was London's first, and locally it was followed by the Regent's Canal in 1820), as well as factories, gasworks and breweries. Gone were the merchants of the past, and the population was predominantly working class.

However, in the north was a significant open space, created by government in 1845: Victoria Park. This was London's first new park of the century and consisted of nearly 300 acres. Initially there were hopes that this would be part of a middle-class suburb.

The docks and industry were stimulated by the better transport links, such as the London and Blackwall Railway in 1840 and the North London

Railway in 1850. The East Counties Railway ran though the district as far as Shoreditch by 1840 but there was no station locally until the 1870s. There were also new roads and canals linking the docks to their markets and sources of raw materials.

Some industries which had previously flourished were now in decline. Silk weaving was in depression, with foreign competition leading to factories moving elsewhere. What remained of the clothing trade was small-scale workshops reliant on 'sweated labour'. The houses of the wealthy were sold as their owners moved out and were subdivided for poorer residents. There was also some decline in the docks, as the St Katharine Docks were deemed too small for the modern and larger shipping so the company relocated most of its business to the new and larger Victoria Dock after 1864, which was further eastwards.

In Bow and Bromley there were myriad industries: a distillery, a calico works, dye works, and many other noxious trades along the river. Bryant and May was a large factory making matchsticks, which was the subject of a famous strike by the female employees in 1888. But as elsewhere, many firms were small scale and people worked at home.

All this overcrowding created slum conditions for the impoverished masses, many of whom were poor immigrants from Eastern Europe, mainly Jewish. Around Artillery Lane there were 176 houses and these were lived in by 2,516 people. However, it was Bethnal Green that was first identified as the worst suburb in the district, with 82,000 people in small cottages there in 1851. A health reformer noted in 1848, 'the enormous number of dwellings which have been constructed in defiance of every law and principle on which the health and lives of occupants depend'. Water supply was infrequent. Attempts were made by philanthropic movements and religious organisations, both Christian and non-Christian, to alleviate the lot of the locals. Better housing, piecemeal as it was, was one practical result. Andrew Mearn's *Bitter Cry of Outcast London*, published in 1883, gave greater publicity to the disgrace of slum life.

Life was not unremittingly grim. Hoxton became known for its music halls, such as MacDonalds in 1864 and the Varieties of 1870. Pollock's Toy Theatre Shop also opened at this time.

In 1889 there was a major reorganisation of local government in which the county councils were created. In London this entailed the creation of a new county; the County of London, administered by the London

County Council (LCC). This new body held authority over inner London from Hammersmith in the west to Poplar in the east, both north and south of the Thames. In 1900 the metropolitan boroughs were created to govern at the lower tier of local government. In the East End these were Shoreditch (including Haggerston and Hoxton), Poplar (including Bow and Bromley and the Isle of Dogs), Stepney (including Spitalfields, Mile End, Limehouse, Whitechapel, Ratcliff and Shadwell) and Bethnal Green. The latter was keen to assert its civic identity with a town hall being erected in 1909 as well as other public buildings such as wash houses and libraries.

The Twentieth-Century East End

Despite the overcrowding of the nineteenth century, the population resident in the districts which made up the East End increased further in the first few decades of the twentieth century. In 1921 there were 117,238 people in the 760 acres of Bethnal Green, 162,618 in the rather

Stanley Atkinson, Stepney councillor (photo taken by the author, 2017).

less dense Poplar of 2,321 acres, Shoreditch had 104,248 in 658 acres, whilst Stepney had 249,657 people in 1,767 acres. The latter was the fifth highest populated London borough, but only the sixteenth in acreage.

Between the world wars the East End had a reputation for being leftward leaning, which manifested itself in various ways. The council of Poplar were gaoled for their refusal to set a rate which they saw as unfair in their distribution. Bethnal Green Council called a housing estate after the founder of the Soviet Union, Lenin. Lower down the social scale, workers and Jews barricaded the streets in response to a planned Fascist march in 1936 through the East End, which was then stopped, and the subsequent clashes between police and protestors were called the Battle of Cable Street.

The LCC had greater resources than the boroughs and was enthusiastic in its attempts to improve housing conditions in the East End. Some notorious slums such as Bethnal Green's 'Old Nichol' had already been replaced by the Boundary Street Estate. There were also two major schemes of slum clearance in Wapping by the docks in these years. During the Blitz of 1940–1, bombing of London was at its most severe in the East End, especially around the strategically significant Docks. After the destruction caused by bombing during the Second World War, further schemes of slum clearance took place. Radical reconstruction occurred along the recommendations of the Abercrombie County of London Plan. Some of this new housing was quite bleak, and much of the surviving East End was destroyed in the planners' zeal to create a new utopia.

The Stepney-Poplar development plan saw the establishment of several neighbourhood areas across the two boroughs. The old dense street layouts were abandoned and were destroyed if the bombers had not already done that. In theory there would be more open spaces and better housing. This was partially achieved, but rebuilding was often piecemeal and spread over decades. Such comprehensive clearance schemes were discontinued by the 1970s.

Most of the housing built in the post-war years was flats, not houses. There was disagreement over the quality of these new dwellings. The *Picture Post* magazine, in 1949, came out in favour, describing them in glowing terms: these new flats contained 'four rooms, a utility room, a dry balcony, a sun balcony, and a boiler in the kitchen to provide domestic hot water, or else gas or electric water heaters. All living rooms will have open fires.' In conclusion, 'What a contrast to the rooms painted by Charles Dickens'. An architectural critic, though, referred to 'the grim concrete barracks recently provided for the people of Bethnal Green'. The Lansbury estate flats in Poplar won popular approval, too, with new residents being impressed with the new flats. Mrs Alice Snoddy remarked, 'Our new place is just a housewife's dream ... It's the sort of home to be proud of'. After all, many had been living in just one room.

Some East Enders moved out of London after 1945. One destination was the newly built housing estate at Debden in Essex, about half an hour by bus away. Many, though, wanted to stay, citing the fact that their grandparents and parents lived there and that they had been born and bred there. A sociological study concluded that what struck the outsider was that there was 'a sense of community ... a sense of history ... a kinship system. These are all independent variables, and yet in this district they are closely connected in such a way that reinforces each other'. Many thought that the new towns lacked the sense of community enjoyed in the East End. Population declined, with Bethnal Green's 130,000 in 1901 being 58,000 in 1951.

St James' church, Bethnal Green (collection of John Coulter).

However, there were still pockets of slums in the East End in the later 1950s, as an observer noted:

> It was simply appalling. The slums were worse than I could ever have imagined ... The condemned buildings were still standing, nearly 20 years after they had been scheduled for demolition, and were still being lived in. A few old people who could not get away remained, but mostly the occupants were prostitutes, homeless immigrants, drunks or meths drinkers, and drug addicts.

Most of the new housing occurred in Poplar, Bethnal Green and Stepney. Much of the older fabric of Whitechapel remained, partly because many of the buildings here were for commercial, not residential use and so there was no need for rebuilding. Towards the end of the century, in Mile End, some of the tower blocks were demolished and were replaced by low-rise housing in yellow brick, known as the Ocean estate. Spaces free from buildings were transformed by new landscaping and so the district regained a little of its once attractive character.

In 1965 there was another reorganisation of London local government which led to an expansion of London and the amalgamation of the counties of Middlesex and London to form Greater London, with a new governing body, the Greater London Council (GLC). At local level, boroughs were amalgamated, so there were fewer of them but they were larger. Stepney, Poplar and Bethnal Green became the London Borough of Tower Hamlets, so named after the name given to the suburbs to the east of the Tower of London in the sixteenth century. Shoreditch was incorporated into the new London Borough of Hackney. At the same time the Inner London Education Authority (ILEA) was established.

The GLC was abolished in 1986 and the ILEA in 1990. In both cases powers, especially over housing and education, wielded by these bodies were devolved to borough level. In 1999 the Greater London Authority (GLA) was formed, but with less powers than the GLC or LCC.

The East End never stands still. In the later twentieth century there was a reaction to previous housing reforms. The new conservation movement, one example being the Spitalfields Historic Buildings Trust, founded in 1977, aimed at saving the remaining eighteenth-century buildings and nineteenth-century terraces, by having them repaired and reclaimed for domestic use. Former workshops and warehouses were refurbished as housing. One major development was the Docklands, which replaced the now redundant docks, which, as with much industry locally, had declined in the twentieth century. The London Docklands Development Corporation was established in 1981 and the designated 'enterprise zone' on the Isle of Dogs encouraged investors as planning restrictions were simplified. The Canary Wharf development on the site of the former West India Docks became a centre of international business with its office towers and imaginative new waterscape. Better transport links, such as the Docklands Light Railway, the City Airport and the extended Jubilee line made the place far more accessible from the late 1980s onwards.

However, some saw these new commercial and residential developments as quite out of keeping with the general atmosphere of the East End. 'Gentrification' had its critics and 'Mug a Yuppie' was an example of local graffiti. Despite all the progress made in the district in the later nineteenth and twentieth centuries, the borough of Tower Hamlets was, at the end of the latter century, ranked the sixth most socially deprived district in England. It was also one of the most socially diverse, in part

Old and new East End (photo by the author).

because of the influx of people from Bangladesh arriving from the 1970s onwards.

This is only a very brief summary of the history of the districts which make up the East End. There are a number of books which will shed further light on the topic. These include general surveys of London which were published from the sixteenth century onward, such as Stow's *History* and the late eighteenth-century multi-volume *Environs of London* by the Revd Daniel Lysons. There are also histories of individual parishes and of the East End in general (noted in this book's bibliography). Most of these should be fairly easily available at the appropriate local history centres and online book shops. One useful website is www.mernick.org.uk/thal. However, no website or book can be a complete account, focusing in detail of every aspect of a local history, and for that information you will need to delve into what are known as primary sources and we shall now explore these topic by topic.

Chapter 2

WORKING LIVES IN THE EAST END

Walter Besant wrote, at the end of the nineteenth century that, despite great poverty,

> East London is ... above all things the city of the working man – the greatest city of the respectable working man in the whole world. Fortunately he is, for the most part, in good and steady work ... The great mass of the population consists of the steady craftsmen, with the foremen and the managers of departments, and the clerks employed in the factories and the works. (*East London*, 1901, p. 22)

Hours of work for our ancestors, when they were not unemployed, were long. This is certainly true of the East End. It is therefore important that we know something about what they did for work. The basic sources for family history, namely parish registers, certificates of civil registration and the census returns, should be the first port of call, since for the nineteenth and twentieth centuries these will be of great help in identifying what their employment was. But this is just the first step.

Records of Companies

There were numerous industries in the East End in the nineteenth and twentieth centuries, as has already been noted. Some of the great many companies that have operated in the East End have left records behind which can now be viewed at various record offices. Only a minority of their archives survive, and those that do vary immensely in what exists, in terms of the date range and the type of material. For James Latham's Shoreditch company, which imported timber, only the trade catalogues which the firm produced survive (at Hackney Archives, hereafter HA) and then only from 1935–7. At the other end there is Bryant and May, whose company archives survive from 1852 to 1977 and include long runs of the minutes of directors' meetings, general meetings, shareholders' meetings and executive committee meetings. There are also annual reports, correspondence, catalogues, advertising material, financial papers, in-house magazines, and records of production and public relations. There is enough to be able to write a very comprehensive history, as well as being informative about former employees, whereas the archives for James Latham's firm would certainly not enable such a tome to be produced.

Of prime interest for the family historian are the records of employees, as these should give name, occupation, salary and dates of commencement and leaving, as well as changes in status and pay. Those held at HA are as follows:

1. Norman and Sons, Ltd, Shoreditch (footwear wholesalers), D/B/NOR: Staffing records, 1941–60
2. Bryant and May Ltd, Fairfield Works, Bow (matchstick manufacturers), D/B/BRY: Staffing records, 1852–1960 (closed for 75 years) and the house magazines, 1921–68. Also see below.
3. J and W Nicholson & Co., Ltd, Bow and Poplar (distillers), D/B/NIC: Employee and staff records, 1852–73, 1878–1913, 1967–8
4. John Carter and Sons, Ltd, Kingsland Road, Shoreditch (boot and shoe makers), N/B/CAR: Wages and pension records, 1887–1946
5. Richard Pye and Sons, Ltd, Shoreditch (box makers), D/B/PYE: Photographs and drawings of staff, 1945–54

At THLHL&A (Tower Hamlets Local History Library and Archives) are the following:

1. Bryant and May: Brymay Magazines, 1921–1977, LC1544.
2. J J and S W Chalk, Timber Merchants and importers, Limehouse and Whitechapel: Wage books (listing names of employees and salary), 1930–82 and other employee records, c.1894–1974, B/CHA/3.
3. G W Mancell, Ltd, iron and steel merchants, Cahir Street, B/MAN/4: Wage books, 1929–37.

LONDON LIFE: The Busy Docks in the Port of London.
London Docks (collection of the author).

4. Trueman, Hanbury, Buxton & Co., Ltd, Spitalfields: Black Eagle, annual publication, 1929–38, LC1545.

There are many other works magazines at THLHL&A in the pamphlets collection, but the runs are often limited in number.

An example of a wages book from the above mentioned Chalks lists employees by function – office staff, drivers, labourers and cleaner – giving names, amounts due in net and gross, deductions and employer's national insurance contributions, per week, showing when the employee began and left the firm, how much they were paid and their job therein.

It is worth recalling that other company archives may mention your ancestors, staff magazines in particular. Brymay's quarterly magazine included information about employees on retirement and obituaries, as well as articles written by employees about their interests (on one occasion, antique coins) and about holidays. The activities of sports and social clubs were also reported, often with pictures. An example taken from 1974 includes the following:

> Miss J.M. Liell
> On June 30th, Miss J.M. Liell retired from Book Match sales, after 30 years service.
> Joining Match Control in 1944 as a typist, she was transferred in 1949, to Bryant and May, working in the sales Order Department.
> In 1965 she was made a supervisor. With the introduction of mechanised accounting, and the revision of the sales order system in 1969, she was transferred to the Book Match Sales Department, where she was employed as a contract Records Clerk until her retirement.

An obituary was as follows:

> Mr Leonard Ernest Reid
> On May 15th, aged 81. Mr Reid was Manager of the British Match Corporation's Statistical Department when he retired in 1959 after 40 years' service.

Apart from these, other archives of the business may also be worth reading for, though they may not mention your ancestor/s, they may help you to understand the nature of the business that they were employed in. Minutes of directors will tell you what the company's aims were and how they tried to achieve these, which almost certainly will have affected

Cloth Market, Goulston Street (collection of Lindsay Siviter).

the workforce and thus your ancestors. There may also be details of the products made and the methods used.

Maritime Trades

Because several of the East End parishes adjoin the northern side of the Thames close to the Docks, it is not surprising that many men earned their living in trades connected to ships and the sea. The West India Dock Company was one the major nineteenth-century employers. Many dock workers were employed and paid on a day-to-day basis, working on the hard manual tasks of loading and unloading the cargoes. These men went unrecorded, but some men were employed on a permanent basis. They were the skilled tradesmen and senior employees involved in supervisory, managerial and clerical roles, better paid and, more importantly from our point of view, better recorded.

Records from the nineteenth century and up to 1909 are held in the archives of the relevant companies and at the Museum of London Docklands. West and East India Dock Company records list salaried staff from their inception in 1803 until 1893.

In 1909 the Port of London Authority took over the running of London's docks. They maintained records of permanent manual and skilled workers. These state where and when a man worked, physical descriptions, employment history, family and personal details, references to periods of ill health, promotions and comments on work and character. Records from 1909 to the 1960s are held at the Museum of the Docklands.

Much of dock work was casual; records were not kept of such temporary employees, but a graphic description was given to Jennifer Worth, a midwife in Poplar in the 1950s:

> I tried to get work in the docks. You would think there was plenty of work in London Docklands, wouldn't you? Well, there was, but there were thousands and thousands of men after the same work. I reckon there were ten men for every job – no chance for a young boy like me.
>
> In those days, such jobs as there were went mostly to the boys whose fathers and grandfathers had been dockers, Mr Collett explained. There were frightening scenes at the dock gates: hundreds of half starved labourers, clad in rags, crazed and desperate, fighting for the chance of a few hours' work. Perhaps fifty would be taken on for the day while five hundred would be turned away to idle their time away in the streets. No wonder men were violent.

Many men went out in the ships, of course. A major employer from 1600 to 1856 was the East India Company, which traded in India. Their archives are to be found at the British Library in the Asian Collection. Although there are no overall indexes, there are listings of masters and mates. Ships' logs, of which there are almost 10,000 surviving, list crew members. There is also Farrington's *A Biographical Index of East India Company Maritime Service Officers 1600–1834* (1999). Richard Morgan's *An Introduction to British Ships in Indian Waters* is useful for the period, too.

The Company also provided for widows of employees and the latter when too old or infirm to work. Some of this help was provided in the Poplar almshouses.

For the Merchant Navy, the LMA (London Metropolitan Archives) has a list of petitions from 8,000 of their sailors and their families dating from 1787–1854. These can also be seen in www.originsnetwork.com. On Findmypast.com are lists of merchant seamen from 1835 to 1941 and crew lists from 1861 to 1913. Some muster rolls post-1747 can be found at the Maritime History Archive at Newfoundland University on www.mun.ca/mha/holdings/searchcombinedcrews.php. Ancestry.

co.uk includes masters' and mates' certificates of competence, 1850–1927. Muster books from 1747–1834 can be seen at TNA (The National Archives), BT 98 but do not list all a ship's crew. Better are the crew lists from 1835 to 1994 at TNA, BT99, which provide more information about an individual's service but are not all complete. Medal rolls for merchant seamen during both world wars can be viewed on Ancestry.co.uk. Apprentices indentured to the Merchant Navy from 1824 to 1910 can be found on Ancestry.co.uk, showing name, date of birth, date of indenture and age. The book, *Tracing your Merchant Navy Ancestors* by Simon Wills should be consulted.

Then there was the Royal Navy, a more dangerous, especially in wartime, and less well paid occupation. Records for sailors are held at TNA (The National Archives). Muster rolls listing ships' crews from 1667 to 1878 are to be found in ADM31-9, 115, 117 and 119 and are searchable on TNA's Discovery. More detailed records commence in 1764, when men's ages and birthplaces are given. Ships' pay books list sailors, too.

Sailors were also required to make wills so that any monies owing at time of death could be sent to their heirs. Up to 1858, the PCC (Prerogative Court of Canterbury) records contain many sailors' wills and indexes to these can be accessed online at TNA's website. The Admiralty also maintained registers of service, 1802–94, accessible on Ancestry.co.uk and registers of service can be searched on Discovery, taken from ADM 139, 188, 362–3. Pension records, 1789–1894, can be searched on Discovery and seen at TNA, ADM73. Seamen's wills from 1786 to 1882 can be searched on Ancestry.co.uk.

Many service records, about 600,000, can be seen online at Ancestry.co.uk, for those in the Royal Navy from 1802 to 1919. Medal rolls can also be searched for men earning gallantry awards from 1793 to 1972. References to officers from 1814 can be found in the quarterly Navy Lists, which are indexed and give dates of appointments to various ranks. Some Navy Lists are available on Ancestry.co.uk, but a complete set can be seen on the shelves of TNA's library.

The National Maritime Museum at Greenwich has a listing of all naval officers from 1660 to 1815 and there is a similar listing on Ancestry.co.uk, searchable by name. The 28,000 men who served at the Battle of Trafalgar in 1805 can be identified on the site, www.nationalarchives.gov.uk/trafalgarancestors. *Tracing your Naval Ancestors* by Simon Fowler and the various books about tracing ancestors from the world wars will provide additional guidance.

Other seamen were the watermen and lightermen, plying the River Thames in their boats with passengers or working to take cargoes from large vessels to the shore. This was a trade which often ran in the family as sons followed fathers. The Watermen's Company was founded in 1566 and they were joined by the Lightermen in 1700. Not all such boatmen were registered with these companies, however.

Records of watermen from 1688 to 1908 are held at the LMA. These are broken down as follows: binding books of apprentices, 1688–1908 (CLC/L/WA/C/020/MS06289) and affidavit books of apprentices, 1759–1987 (CLC/L/WA/C/026/MS06291). These provide names of apprentices, date of birth, place of baptism, date of beginning of apprenticeship, name of master and date when the apprentice became a free waterman. It was also possible for older men to become apprentices and the records for these from 1865 to 1926 are at CLC/L/WA/E/017/MS19548A. All these have been indexed. There are also archives of lists of pensioners, 1794–1928, of the inmates of the company almshouses in Penge, 1841–59, listings of Sunday services, 1721–1831, and archives dealing with complaints against watermen; apparently 20 per cent of all watermen were featured therein. The site www.findmypast.co.uk includes Thames watermen from 1865 to 1921.

Many men in the East End worked on the railways. Listings can be found on Ancestry.co.uk of railway workers from 1833 to 1963. These provide names, dates of birth, age, occupation, location of employment, rate of pay and personal remarks. The book, *Tracing your Railway Ancestors*, by Di Drummond should help.

If your ancestor was self-employed, perhaps a shopkeeper, he or she should be listed in the London directories which exist for most of the nineteenth and twentieth centuries and which were produced annually. These can be viewed at the Guildhall Library, TNA, LMA, the Bishopsgate Institute and the two local history centres, as well as on line at www.directorisonline. The information provided here is minimal, as directories provide listings of businesses, with address and type of business, by year. However sometimes there may be an advert for the said business which will give more of an idea of the goods and services offered. Looking at a run of directories can be very useful, for you can

Street market, Petticoat Lane (collection of Lindsay Siviter).

then find out how long it was in existence and whether it moved premises and whether it grew to occupy more or bigger premises, and when/whether it declined.

Another good source for businesses is the local press. This is because many businesses advertised therein. However, looking through unindexed newspapers in the hope that something relevant might turn up is a time-consuming business. That said, a search through digitised newspapers is worth trying; who knows, there might have been more, perhaps a fire or a robbery or an accident taking place which would be reported, or a works outing or other social activity. Apart from local newspapers, do remember to check the *London Gazette*, which can be accessed online at www.thegazette.co.uk for free and searched by keyword. Bankruptcy notices were published here and these will tell you when the company folded and may provide additional information about the owners and receivers.

Businesses often took out insurance on their property and goods. Several firms sprang up in the later seventeenth century, partly as a response to the Great Fire of 1666. Their archives can provide useful information about businesses, although of course, they covered domestic property, too. In some cases, of course, the business was run from the owner's house. The information given in the following sets of registers usually includes the number of the policy, the name/location of the agent, name, status, occupation and address of the policy holder, location of the premises, type and nature of the property, its value, the premium paid and when the renewal was due. Details of any tenants might also be given, if applicable. Fire policy registers exist for the Hand-in-Hand insurance company for 1696–1865 (Ms 8674-8, 166 volumes), the Sun, 1710–1863 (Ms 11936-7, 1,262 volumes) and the Royal Exchange, 1753-9 and 1773–1883 (Ms 7252-5, 173 volumes). All are held at the LMA. If these huge numbers of registers, arranged chronologically, sound daunting, do bear in mind that there are a number of indexes. There is an online name index for the Sun from 1800 to 1839. There is also a card index at the LMA for the Sun's policies between 1714 and 1731 (Ms 17817) and a microfiche index to both Sun and Royal Exchange policies for 1775-87 (Ms 24172). Those for that other major London insurer, The Phoenix, are located at Cambridge University Library.

Records of female employment are limited beyond what is stated on the census returns. One well-known female occupation (by no means the only one) in the East End was prostitution. Those involved in this trade would not attest to it in the census returns, but will feature in court registers (see chapter 4) where they will be noted as having been fined for practising their trade. It was not a full-time occupation and sometimes women might resort to it in times of poverty, sometimes to feed a dependency on alcohol.

Those who were self-employed often advertised in the local press. This was often the case for schoolmasters and schoolmistresses in the nineteenth century, when there were myriad small schools. There were also tutors who would specialise in a particular subject, such as music or foreign languages. The adverts would often state the qualifications and experience of the teacher, as well as laying out what they would teach, the ages and sex of pupils sought, as well as the address where they would be taught (often at the teacher's own home). Such adverts often appeared on the front page of nineteenth-century press.

Public Sector Employment

In the nineteenth century the number of people employed by the public sector grew phenomenally. This was especially the case with local government, which by the late nineteenth century began to employ

Shops on Petticoat Lane (collection of Lindsay Siviter).

salaried officials, both professional and manual employees. This was because central government took an increasingly interventionist role and, following reforming legislation, especially in matters of health and education, it was the task of local government to employ people to carry out the wishes of Parliament. Councils were run by elected representatives which met en bloc about once a month, but increasingly much of the work was done by committees; dealing with matters such as Finance, Works (infrastructure and planning), Housing, Libraries, Parks and so on. Each have their separate series of minute books, arranged chronologically and sometimes indexed. By the twentieth century these will be typed but for the previous century, expect them to be hand written.

Council and committee minutes are full of references to the senior officials such as the town clerk, the surveyor, borough librarian and so on, as these were prominent in committee meetings in their advisory roles and will often be reported as such in the local press, too. Local newspapers in the nineteenth and early twentieth centuries often reported council meetings in great detail, referring to the contributions in debates and reports by councillors and relevant senior officials.

However, even relatively junior employees, such as lady typists, dust collectors and scavengers, and assistants to more senior men, often merit inclusion in council and committee minutes. Permanent employees will usually be mentioned when they commence employment and when they cease. They may be mentioned at other times, such as if there is a change in pay, an exceptional period of illness or an accident or a misdemeanour. However, as a minimum, you should be able to find when they started work, their job title/department and salary, when/why they left and possibly pension arrangements.

Annual Returns of the borough councils are a useful source if your ancestor was one of the elected representatives of the people. Those for Poplar (1900–38) list councillors, their addresses and which committees they were members of. Stepney Year Books (1900–65) also note which ward councillors represented and how many votes they received at the last election for which they stood. Times and dates of committee meetings are also noted here so you would know what your councillor ancestor was doing on particular evenings. Senior council officers of the departments are also listed therein. These books can be found on the shelves of THLHL&A's library. Registers of Stepney Council staff and published lists of Poplar council employees can be seen here, too.

THLHL&A holds a number of registers of employees of certain sections of the councils' staffs. These are as follows. Central Foundation Girls' School, 1898–1968, includes notes of absence (I/CFS/A/2/4/3-6); George Green School, Poplar, 1908–28 (ACC/1811-1 and 3 (LMA)); Bethnal Green Library staff sickness pay, 1962–5 (l/BGM/F/4/2); Stepney Town Clerk's department, 1900–65 (L/SMB/B/4/1–6); Whitechapel Library, attendance, 1955–99 (L/THL/H/2/5/1); Wapping Library attendance, 1971–80 (L/THL/H/2/7/3); Bancroft Library, 1965–1986, and Tower Hamlets Music Library Staff registers, 1970–1986 (THL/H/4/1/2–4).

Bethnal Green's Board of Guardians' printed minutes from 1919–30 are useful if your ancestor was a Guardian or a member of staff employed by them. The minutes frequently refer to staff taken on or leaving and provide brief details which are available nowhere else. On 5 February 1924, Florence Brooks, aged 29, was appointed as a ward attendant on the South Ambulance and Receiving Ward at the rate of 51 shillings per week and a uniform. On 19 April 1924 we learn that Alice Ellen Douglas Heale was a probationer nurse who had completed her training with them. She was now leaving with a certificate stating that her conduct had been 'Good' and her work had been 'Satisfactory'. Leave of absence was also noted, as in the following example, concerning Florence Nightingale (named after the famous nurse of Crimean War fame): 'We recommend that the above named housemaid be granted rations allowance at the appropriate rate for the period during which she was allowed to go away on sick leave recently, following an attack of pleurisy'. Returns of temporary staff – including porters, scrubbers, attendants and labourers but also butchers, bakers and barbers – occur frequently, too, giving names, dates, position and wages. None of these books are indexed by staff name, so searching through them can be a lengthy business.

Such printed minute books exist for Bethnal Green, 1919–30, Poplar, 1893–1914, Whitechapel, 1891–1914, and Stepney, 1925–30. They can be found on the shelves of THLHL&A's library. Further reference to these will be found in chapter 3, where their work is examined. The original manuscript minute books are at LMA; local libraries collected printed copies and hence their existence at THLHL&A.

Workhouse staff are well recorded. For Bethnal Green's Waterloo House Workhouse there are staff record papers, 1919–35, and staff appointment registers, 1880–98 (BEBG/348). The same union also ran Leytonstone Children's Home – with staff registers, 1878–98 (BEBG/349/1–3) and 1919–37, registers of nurses and house mothers, 1917–31, and of outdoor staff, 1909–31. There are also registers of staff resignations, 1896 and 1930–5, registers of staff appointments, 1875–1930, indexed from 1894 to 1930, and records of officers who left the service in 1927 only.

For Whitechapel Union there are registers of staff and officers from 1857 to 1925 (STBG/WH/147/1–80) and a register of their testimonials from 1901 to 1925 (STBG/WH/148), the latter arranged alphabetically. All these staff records are available at the LMA, as are all post-1834 workhouse records.

There are also specific records relating to council staff. Shoreditch Council had a Staffing Committee in 1920–7 and 1935–64 (S/G/1-26; S/GJ/3), and this will discuss issues relevant to staff, pay, holidays and working conditions. These archives are held with the appropriate record office, so those for the London Borough of Tower Hamlets and its predecessor bodies (Stepney, Bethnal Green and Poplar Borough Councils) are held at THLHL&A. Those for Shoreditch Vestry, later

Borough Council, and its successor body, the London Borough of Hackney, are held at HA.

Employees of central government, such as the Post Office and the Police Forces, are relatively easy to research. The former can be found at the Royal Mail Archives using Pensions ledgers, which are indexed and provide a brief overview of the employee's career. For the police, archives of the Metropolitan Police can be found at TNA under joiners, 1830–57 and 1878–1933 (MEPO4/333–8), leavers, 1889–1947 (MEP04/339–51), pensions, 1852–1923 (MEPO21) and those who died in service, 1829–99 (MEPO4/2). Those for the City of London Police are located at the LMA and are arranged alphabetically by surname. On Ancestry.co.uk, you can check the Metropolitan police pension registers for 1852–1932. Stephen Wade's *Tracing your Police Ancestors* would be helpful, too.

Senior police officers, once retired, often write their memoirs and these usually include information about their career progress as well as their famous cases. Former Chief Inspector Walter Dew's memoirs, *I Caught Crippen* (1938), include details of his early career as a constable in the East End in the late 1880s and early 1890s (he discusses his minor role in the Ripper investigation). Thomas Divall's memoirs, *Scoundrels and Scallywags* (1929) are also of an officer who served in the East End at this time and these shed a light on the role of the East End copper and so are of obvious relevance to anyone whose ancestor served in the police in this district.

Newspapers are a good source of information, especially if there is 'trouble at the mill'. One of the most famous industrial disputes in the East End was the match girls' strike at Bryant and May, covered by the local and national press. If your ancestor was one of the famous matchgirls, then the reporting of the strike is a key moment for your family history. As an example here is the following article in *The Times* newspaper of 10 July 1888:

> THE MATCH GIRLS' STRIKE
>
> This strike last evening assumed a new phase. Many of the girls openly expressed their desire to return to their work, and their opinion that it would be best for all to do so. They said they had nothing to fall back upon, and the three days' money they took on Saturday was all expended. Some of them said that they had no breakfast, and that people would not trust them with either food or lodgings while out

Bryant and May factory (photo by Paul Lang).

of work. After all the money that had been collected on Saturday and Sunday they thought that those who were really without means would have been allowed some to go on with. There were many young girls who were orphans and had no friends near them. A correspondent had an interview last evening with Messrs Bryant and May and also some of the directors. Mr Frederick Bryant stated that the girls in the wax factory had that morning resumed their work, and had remained at work all day. There had, however, been considerable opposition on the part of some of the match workers to their coming in, and he had been informed that in some instances there had been disputes about it, and in one case, a fight. From the information he had been given he had felt it his duty to get them protection. He had had an interview with the Under Secretary of State and with Sir Charles Warren, and ample protection had been allotted them. In reply to a question as to whether he would take all the strikers back, providing they consented to resume work, he said he was not prepared to say that he would. The women in the Victoria factory were the ringleaders in the strike. It was the hands in that factory that first came out, and he would deal with those in that factory in a way that would make an example of them to the others. Probably this would be by refusing to take any of them on again.

With respect to the girls in the 'Centre' factory, they were drawn off, and he would not refuse to take them on again. Then there were the girls in the safety match manufactory. They also only followed the lead of the others, and he would take them on again also. The Social Democratic Federation have telegraphed to their sections at Glasgow asking them to hold immediately demonstrations against the importation of match girls from Glasgow to London during the strike at Bryant and May's.

Additional information about the female strikers and others involved in industrial action can be found on www.unionancestors.co.uk. Mark Crail's *Tracing your Labour Movement Ancestors* (2009) is recommended.

There were many clergymen in the East End; some vicars in the late nineteenth century had up to four curates. They were generally very busy and hard-working men, involved in the spiritual and physical needs of their parishioners. For clergy up to 1900, the registers of the universities of Oxford, Cambridge and London can be consulted; those for the former two can be searched on Ancestry.co.uk. Anglican clergymen up to 1834

Clock Mill, Bromley by Bow (photo by Paul Lang).

can be found on the Church of England Clergymen's database, www.theclergydatabase.org.uk.

Other sources are *Crockford's Clerical Directory* from 1858, arranged alphabetically by clergy, which provides details of education, career and publications, if any, and published annually (several copies can be searched in Ancestry.co.uk, copies can also be seen at the LMA, TNA and the Guildhall Library). *The Clerical List* of 1842–1917 was another annual publication which listed clergy as was *The Clerical Guides* of 1817, 1822, 1829 and 1836. Parish archives, parish magazines, minute books and other sources to be found at the LMA will also refer to the clergy, as will the local press; churches once advertised their services and special events in the life of the churches were usually recorded. The *Church Times* newspaper is also useful for obituaries.

For other denominations, there is the *Catholic Directory*, published annually from 1850. The *Baptist Handbook* was published in six volumes from 1899 to 1927. Finally there were the *United Methodist Ministers and Circuits* volumes for 1797–1932, organised by circuit and then by clergyman. All these can be seen at the Guildhall Library. Many clergy

Barracks of East London Royal Engineers, Bethnal Green (collection of John Coulter).

wrote autobiographies or had biographies written of them and many can be found on the shelves at THLHL&A.

It is easier to find out about working lives if the place of employment still exists, especially for the public sector or in the case of relatively large firms. For many employees, there is, regrettably, very little information. This is especially the situation for those in casual and part-time employment, such as labouring, sweating crafts, casual dock work and much more. If this is the case, then the best way of finding out about them is to discover what others wrote about that particular branch of employment.

Chapter 3

EAST END POVERTY AND ATTEMPTS AT ITS RELIEF

There is often the impression given that the East End was a pit of universal poverty and despair. Not everyone who lived in the East End was poor, of course. As noted in chapter 1, until the early nineteenth century and afterwards, there were numerous well-to-do people in the East End villages. Yet in the nineteenth and twentieth centuries many Eastenders undoubtedly did feel the economic pinch and at the dawn of the current century the London Borough of Tower Hamlets is one of the poorest places in Britain. This chapter examines how we can find information about our ancestors who fell on hard times in the East End, by examining both the two main forms of attempts to relieve poverty (public and private) and looking at contemporary accounts of poverty, both written by middle-class outsiders and, in the twentieth century, East Enders themselves, recounting their lives. A general book worth consulting is *Tracing your Pauper Ancestors* by Robert Burlison.

It is certainly possible to produce a great deal of evidence about poverty in the East End in the nineteenth and twentieth centuries, though much the same could be said about many other parts of England, too. For the nineteenth century, as far as impressions go, there are many from journalists and social reformers, rather than the poor of the East End themselves. Jack London, an American author, was writing about the poor in London at the beginning of the twentieth century and one of his vignettes was of the dining room of a common lodging house which he visited near Middlesex Street, Whitechapel:

Here and there, at the various tables, other men were eating, just as silently. In the whole room there was hardly a note of conversation. A feeling of gloom pervaded the ill lighted place. Many of them sat and brooded over the crumbs of their repast, and made me wonder … what evil they had done that they should be punished so. (*The People of the Abyss*, 1903, pp. 277–8)

The Poor Law (Old and New)

The statutory form of poor relief was initially the Old Poor Law, which was codified in 1601 and lasted until 1834. This stated that the relief of poverty was the responsibility of the parish, which would collect money from parishioners, known as rates, and then redistribute it as either cash or in kind (food, clothes, fuel) to the needy, principally those too young, too old or too infirm or ill to undertake paid work. Some payments were made on a semi-permanent basis, for example, payments to elderly widows; others were of a temporary nature, for example, to a man who was injured and unable to work, until he was healed. This type of relief

Parochial benefactions of Shoreditch (photo by the author).

was known as outdoor relief as it was given to people as they lived in their own homes. However, parishes could establish workhouses, where the poor could be housed and fed but had to work for their upkeep.

Shoreditch vestry's accounts exist in an incomplete run from 1818 to 1872, rent accounts from 1817 to 1828 (P/L/P/1–2) and there is a casual relief list from 1843 (P/L/P/10). These can be found at HA. The bulk of this parish's poor law archives are held at the LMA, however, and consist of the following; rate books, 1688–1858, settlement and bastardy certificates, 1698–1857 (P91/LEN/1129–1180), orders for removals, 1765–1854, registers of apprentices, 1767–1842 (P91/LEN/1331-1333), workhouse admissions, 1788–1845, register of deaths, 1788–1861 (P91/LEN/1335–46) and of births, 1836–62 (P91/LEN/3-6), lists of children chargeable to the parish, 1829–35 (P91/LEN/1340–1), register of tramps, 1848–50 (P91/LEN1335–9), register of children, 1817–19.

The main sources for family history are the disbursement books for the old poor law. These list payments (in cash or in goods) given by the overseers to those in need, with name of recipient and reason for relief given. Those for Limehouse exist from 1763 to 1773 (L/SAL/3/1), for Poplar from 1825 to 1833 (L/ASP/F/3/3–7), for St Mary's Stratford Bow from 1806 to 1825 (L/SMS/C/8/1–5) and for Bromley, 1667–1831 (L/BSL/D/1/1–3). All are held at THLHL&A. An example of one from Limehouse shows lists of people who were relieved on a regular basis, giving date, name and sum received. For example, on 25 August 1770 Mary Courtneys was given one shilling. Sometimes there are more details, with the reason for the relief given; for example, on 22 May 1773 Susanna Joynes was given £1 7s 'for the maintenance of her child from December'; perhaps she was a single parent.

Parishes were often in dispute with one another over the application of the poor law, especially over the issue of settlement. This dated back to legislation of 1662. The poor could only claim relief if they had been born in the parish where they were making a claim, had married someone who had rights in the parish or had lived there for a year and paid rates there. Parishes often clashed over who should pay relief. These disputes were resolved at the Middlesex quarter sessions, whose archives are held at the LMA. Sessions books from 1558–1709 have been published and indexed. At THLHL&A are examination papers for Bow (1739–42, 1828–44 and 1859–61 at L/SMS/C/5/1–3), Bromley (1788–1843 at L/

BSL/D/4/1-5) and the Old Artillery Yard (1792–1852 at L/OAG/5/1–3). These give potted biographies of the poor as they were examined by magistrates about their legal settlement in a parish and this eligibility for parish relief.

In order to pay for all this, the parish vestry levied rates, perhaps the modern equivalent might be seen as the council tax, based on property sizes and payable by the owner. Lists of payers and payments due were listed in rate books, an underused source for family history and one which has largely escaped the attention of indexers and digitisers. The lists do not list all in the parish, rather those householders (mostly male) who could pay, but the lists were revised annually and so are a good source to show when your rate-paying ancestors arrived and left and which give a rough idea of their wealth at that stage in their lives, too. Most of the rates went on poor relief, though not all, and the later rate books exist beyond the end of the old poor law in 1834.

The following poor rate books are held at THLHL&A; Bow, 1773–1887 (L/SMS/B/2–89), also church rate books, 1810–62 (L/BSL/B/4/1–4), highway rate books, 1841–55 (L/SMS/B/4/1–5), general rate books, 1856–60 and conjunct rate books, 1860–99, Bromley, 1783–1836 (L/BSL/2/1–28), also highway rate books, 1816–42 (L/BSL/3/1–8) and church rate books, 1812–62, (L/BSL/B/4/1–4), Poplar, 1708–1842 (L/ASP/E/3/1–190), also church rate books, 1799–1868 (L/ASP/E/5/1–44) and conjunct rate books, 1813–81; Bethnal Green, 1744 and 1794, also church rate books, 1743–51 (L/MBG/C/2/1), highway rate books, 1791, 1838 and combined rate books, 1787–1882). Purely secular rate books are listed in chapter 10. The summoning book listing rate defaulters for Shoreditch for 1779–1802 can be found on Ancestry.co.uk.

Rate books are often subdivided by street. In the case of Limehouse in the late eighteenth century these were Fore Street, Rhodes Well, Three Colt Street, Limehouse Causeway, Limehouse Corner, Limekiln Hill, Ropemaker's Fields, Rope Walk and Nightingale Lane.

From 1834 to 1930 the New Poor Law was in force and its aim was to increase the efficiency of poor relief. Instead of relief being administered by individual parishes, it was common for several adjoining ones to form together in a poor law union in which to administer it. That said, relief in Shoreditch was managed by the Shoreditch Union. Stepney Board of

Guardians was established in 1836 and it included Limehouse, Mile End, Ratcliff, Shadwell and Wapping. In 1857 a separate Board of Guardians was founded for Mile End, but in 1925 Mile End, St George in the East and Whitechapel were added to the Stepney Union. Other poor law unions in the East End were Bethnal Green, Whitechapel, St George in the East and Poplar.

The New Poor Law was also noted for providing relief to those who entered the workhouses which it created. These were large complexes of buildings where the poor were housed, fed and had to work for their board and lodging, though workhouses had existed previously, on a smaller scale.

Workhouses are often mentioned by those writing their memoirs of life in the East End in the early to mid twentieth century. Jennie Hawthorne, who was a child in the 1920s, recalled:

> The workhouse was always there, its baleful presence glowering in the distance, threatening anybody who gave up the fight to keep body and soul together. When I was taken to see an ageing relative of my mother, I remember the atmosphere of despair and desolation, the dreary clothes, the compulsive wandering of inmates round the bit of grey yard, like trained but captive animals who had given up all hopes of release. (*East End Memories*, 2005, p. 120)

Some of the archives created by these unions include admission and discharge registers, which list inmates' date of admission and departure, with name, age and 'Remarks'. Whilst the first three are self-explanatory, the final one is a comment about matters surrounding the inmate's departure; for the Shoreditch Workhouse, they include, 'To Enfield', 'Died', 'To service', 'With 5s[hillings] and a pair of shoes' and 'With the mother'. For Elizabeth Andrews, aged 71, who entered this workhouse on 20 January 1826 and left on 29 March 1827, she left 'with shirt'.

Porters' registers note more details in the rare eventuality of their survival. For the Poplar Workhouse, these include time as well as date of arrival, name, age, marital status, occupation, creed, date of discharge and name and address of friends. An example is as follows. Charles Cook was admitted at five past twelve on 4 August 1917. He was single, aged 27, a carman, Church of England. He was discharged at a quarter to two on 7 August 1917 to his sister, Mrs Griffin of 28 Juniper Street, Shadwell.

Children's registers tend to provide additional information: date of entry, name, religious denomination, year of birth, parish of origin, date discharged and method of discharge. One example from the Limehouse Children's establishment is as follows: Henry Elliott, admitted 5 April 1870, born in 1858, Church of England, admitted from the parish of Limehouse, discharged at father's request, the father being from Bromley.

Lunatic registers list dates of admission and discharge, name and 'observations'. In one instance for the Bethnal Green institution we learn that John Peter was admitted on 14 March 1889 and discharged on 28 October 1890. It was noted that he had been transferred from Hoxton House.

Creed registers list name of inmate, date of admission and discharge, date of birth, last address prior to admittance, creed and where transferred to on departure. An example from Shoreditch Workhouse is Alfred Butcher who was admitted on 1 August 1917. He had been born on 1 February 1914 and had previously lived at 76 Laburnum Street. He was Church of England and was discharged on 2 August 1917 to the Cottage Homes.

Pauper registers list dates of admission and discharge, name, year of birth, creed, occupation, name and address of friends. A Shoreditch example is of James Bancroft, admitted on 9 January 1909 and discharged 2 February 1909. He had been born in 1842, was Church of England, was a boot closer and named Mrs Warren of 10 Warren Street as next of kin.

Settlement and relief books do have a contemporary index to names and the information provided therein varies considerably. For example, the Bethnal Green Settlement book for 1855–6 states 'Eliz Newman 56 an inmate can't make anything of her. She has lost her speech. Casual'. A rather fuller statement is made for the next inmate:

> Isabella Vachee 53 an inmate. She was married 1821 or 1822 at St. James' Pickadilly, no certificate to husband Anthony Vachee now absent from her. Merchants clerk 5 feet 9 inches high dark eye. Brown hair. About six months after marriage husband took house No. 13 Jubilee Mile End of Mr Dumsay landlord at the yearly rate of £23 p. ann besides taxes and occupied same for about 6 months then took house corner John Street and Baker Street of Mr Cohen agent to Mr Auchtimore at the yearly rent of 30 Guineas per ann, lived 2 years or thereabouts.

Principal poor law archives held at the LMA

Name	Bethnal Green	Poplar	Shoreditch	Stepney
Admission and Discharge Books	1919–35	1845–71, 1902–24, 1928–30	1832–1905	
Apprenticeships	1928		1858–1910	
Births	1878–1926	1837–1914	1862–1921	
Burials	1895–1935	1860–1931		
Children's Registers	1897–1929	1850–75, 1884–1924		1873–1927
Creed Registers	1869–1935	1844–1940	1869–1923	
Deaths	1895–1935	1860–1931		
Inmate Registers	1857–1915			
Lunatic Registers (Asylum)	1838–1914		1863–1908	1871–1927
Lunatic Registers (Workhouse)	1896–1913	1857–86		1871–1927
Pauper Registers	1897–1915			
Reception Orders		1851–1905		1872–1911
Removal Orders	1837–1916	1874–1927	1868–1930	1850–1927
Examination Papers			1887–1918	
Settlement Papers	1839–1917	1885–97		
Admission Orders of Lunatics			1858–1930	1872–1911
Register of Deserted Children	1897–1929		1870–87	1889–1924
Reports of Children Chargeable			1885–1904	
Register of Visitors to Inmates		1900–30	1876–1909	
Register of Relief to Families of Internees		1914–20	1914–20	

Name	Whitechapel	Mile End	St George in the East
Admission and Discharge Books	1908–1926	1847–1921	1811–43, 1854–6
Apprenticeships		1857–1924	

Births	1905–26		1900–21
Burials			
Children's Registers	1871–1927		1866–8, 1887–1927
Creed Registers	1881–1925	1883–1912	
Deaths	1866–9		
Inmate Registers			
Lunatic Registers	1838–1914	1875–1927	1859–1926
Pauper Registers			
Reception Orders		1851–1920	1901–21
Removal Orders	1871–1924	1848–1922	1876–1925
Lunatic Admissions	1901–26		
Lunatic Detention Certificates (Children)	1916–32		
Settlement Papers	1839–1903	1860–75, 1894–1908	1828–36
Lunatic Detention Certificates	1910–14		
Admission Orders, Imbecile Adults	1906–25		
Admission Orders, Imbecile Children	1919–30		

Many of the records mentioned have been digitised and these can usually be searched by name. The principal Poor Law archives held at LMA are listed in the table. Some of these are available on Ancestry.co.uk. For Poplar these are as follows: examination papers 1885–97, removals 1874–1922, and settlement papers 1885–1904. For Bethnal Green these are: examination papers 1839–1903, removals 1837–1916, and settlement papers 1889–1917. For Shoreditch these are examination papers 1908–18, removals 1760–1923, and settlement papers 1698–1917. Finally for Stepney there are removal papers from 1828–36 only. These are not searchable by name, but there are indexes at the beginning of each volume.

There were also children's homes for orphans or those whose parents could not look after them or had been abandoned. Bethnal Green established the Leytonstone Children's Home, whose archives are at the LMA. These include admission and discharge registers 1915–37, creed registers 1876–1937, baptism registers 1928–36, birth certificates 1901–14, death registers 1869–1935, and relatives' address book 1898–1922.

Stepney had Stifford House Children's Home, for which exist admission and discharge registers 1902–31, creed registers 1902–31 and copies of birth certificates 1890–4. Poor law infirmaries are dealt with in chapter 9.

Local newspapers, which reported the activities of public bodies, can be useful source of information about the workhouses in three principal aspects. First, they usually report on the regular meetings of the administrators, namely the Boards of Guardians, who were elected to appoint the officials and then to supervise their activities. These can give an indication as to how these places were run and the intentions/policies in place. Any unusual deaths, such as suicides, accidents and epidemics, which resulted in inquests would be reported. These often give incidental background details about life and routines in the workhouses. Scandals were often reported, such as the following episode, which concerned the Bethnal Green Workhouse, and in particular Theodore Meyrick, the master, and two inmates, Sarah Skinner and Sarah Moss, and was reported in the *East London Observer* over a number of issues; the extract here is taken from the edition of 11 October 1860 and is of part of the inspector's report:

> For some considerable time past, rumours have prevailed in this parish, and stories have been afloat, the effect of which was to cast doubt in the conduct and management of this institution, and implicating the conduct also of the chief officer paid to control it. The rumours at length assumed a more definite form, and at length it was alleged that an inmate of this workhouse had given birth to a child of which she said the master of the workhouse was the father. There was also an allegation against the morality of the master in another case. In the first case it was said that proceedings were instituted with a view to obtaining an affiliation against the master, that these proceedings were not carried to a conclusion in consequence, as was alleged, of a compromise being effected, that money was paid to the woman – money paid to the witnesses – and the legal expenses of the attorney employed to obtain the order was also paid. Whether this was or was not with the knowledge or consent of the master is a question with which we shall have to do thereafter. It is right to say that the Guardians, as soon as the matter assumed a definite form, took up the matter as far as they could. They had it before them, but being in this position – that they had not laid before them sufficient material, and moreover they had no power to compel the attendance of any witnesses, or if they did attend to examine or cross examine

them on oath – all they can do was to have the master before them, and ask him if there was any foundation to the charge. The master denied – most emphatically denied – and still denies that there are any foundations for the rumour; it being the position I have said could not do more, though doubtless the proceedings was unsatisfactory to them, as it was to numbers of the ratepayers. Upon this a number of ratepayers memorialised the poor law board on the subject, and since more than one memorial has been addressed to them.

Finally, there would be special days for the inmates of the workhouse, such as Christmas Day, when they would have different food and entertainments as well as religious instruction. Days out occasionally provided treats in the lives of inmates, sometimes being given by philanthropic bodies, and these were often reported. Of course these events should not be taken as commonplace; after all, newspapers report what is unusual, not what is routine.

The *Shoreditch Observer* reported on 24 February 1900:

> Another excellent concert was given at the workhouse on Tuesday evening organised by Mrs Simons, the event being an unqualified success. Mr W.E. Hinton (vice chairman of the Board of Guardians) presided, and met with a hearty reception from the large audience of old people assembled in the dining hall. Mr Simon contributed several capital songs, and a prominent part was taken by the Misses Langton, of All Saints' Vicarage, Haggerston, who have for several years visited the workhouse weekly to read to and interest the old people, amongst whom they are very popular. The Master and Matron spared no effort to ensure the success of the concert and after votes of thanks to the performers, and the chairman, the interesting gathering closed with the National Anthem.

Minute books and annual reports of the Boards of Guardians are another valuable source for the history of the workhouses, their masters, their employees and their inmates. Many of these printed books for the twentieth century are held on the shelves of THLHL&A, but fuller and earlier minute books and so on are at the LMA. It is worth noting that not all outdoor relief ceased in 1834. The Poplar Union provided outdoor relief and a payments book for 1859–65 can be viewed at THLHL&A (L/SMS/C10/1).

There were other attempts by parishes to assist the poor. For example, there was a Poplar chapel clothing fund, which created a register for the years 1871–1924, listing applicants and clothing given to them, P88/MTS/052. St Matthias' Maternal Society had a register of loans of linen to expectant mothers from 1881 to 1924 at P88/MTS/053. All these are held at the LMA. Parishes were also involved in the distribution of charitable funds. For St Mary Stratford le Bow there are applications for charity pensions from 1912 to 1932 at THLHL&A, L/SMS/F/4/6.

There are also biographical studies of those who were in the receipt of relief, which can give a subjective view of their experiences in the workhouse. *From Workhouse to Westminster: The Life Story of William Crooks, MP*, by George Haw, was published in 1907. There are also a number of studies of the operation of the poor law in the East End; these are listed in the bibliography and can be viewed at the THLHL&A library.

Private Charities

The scale of poverty in the East End in the eighteenth and more especially the nineteenth century led to a great wakening of conscience among some. State efforts were bolstered by the work of charitable individuals. Whilst this occurred in many places, the East End of London was a particularly favoured recipient for such projects which often aimed to better the housing of the poor.

Charities existed in order to assist the poor. Wealthy men and women often left money in their wills to buy property to provide an income to use to ameliorate the lot of the poor. The parish often appointed trustees to oversee these funds. The Shoreditch charity trustees' records (P/L/C) exist at HA for 1745–1900 and these were taken over by the borough from 1901 to 1967.

Two major charities were the George Fournier Charity, for which there exist, at THLHL&A (L/MBG/F/1), receipts and disbursements and signatures of recipients and trustees, some with ages (up to 1869) and addresses of the former. The archives are arranged chronologically from 1842 to 1934. One such recipient was Sarah Carew, aged 77, of 317 Bethnal Green Road, who was given 10s. There is also the Colvill Hall Charity for the parish of St George in the East, established under Prisca Coborn's will. This includes records held at THLHL&A, from 1828

Geffrye Almshouses, Shoreditch, 2017 (photo by the author).

to 1881 (L/SMS/F/1–2) and for 1860 (L/SMS/i/2/4) and includes applications from 130 widows of seamen. These can be viewed online at https://www.ideastore.co.uk/local-history-archives-online-gifts-to-seamen-widows-1860.

The East London Mission and Relief Society was a religious body which helped with relief and its annual reports for 1893–1934 (LC6949, L898) can be viewed at THLHL&A. These reports list subscribers and amounts given, list the committee members and addresses, and give an account of the relief given to the poor. There is a reference to goods accepted for rummage sales, for cheap clothing, and assistance with fuel, the coal club, the penny bank, soup distribution, Mothers' Meetings and the Girls' Own society. Individuals helped are not named, but examples are given, such as:

> LM and FM, two children out of a family of eleven, only one in work (that a girl) had to find them clothes and boots before they could go to Herne Bay for three weeks.

There are archives of other charities, but most do not list recipients and so are of limited interest to family historians, unless your ancestor was the founder of the charity or one of the trustees appointed to administer it. Parish churches often have boards listing parish charities or they can be found by checking the online catalogues for THLHL&A and HA. The major benefactors are discussed next.

Dr Barnardo's was a charity which began when the young Irishman, Dr Thomas John Barnardo, arrived in Stepney and was moved by the plight of children sleeping rough. He began to give them shelter and before long established homes for children, the first being for boys at Stepney Causey in 1870, paid for by donations and subscriptions. Many children went on to learn trades, become apprentices or were sent overseas for, it was hoped, a better life. By 1905, the time of his death, 60,000 children had been helped and the charity still exists to this day. There are a number of books about the founder and his organisation at THLHL&A and the LMA, but some of the deposited archives are held at Liverpool University Library. Others, such as registers of the Stepney Home of Industry, 1870–1920, and the Stepney Home Visitors' Book, 1914–47, are held privately and access is only via TNA's Archive Sector Development. Archives less than a century old are generally closed to researchers. Those seeking ancestors who went through the Barnardo's Homes should contact the organisation for information, at familyhistoryservice@barnardos.org.uk. There is also a sizeable photograph collection of Barnardo's children; about 55,000 exist for 1874–1905, partly created for publicity purposes. Fees are payable for the supply of information and pictures of ancestors.

The Salvation Army was another major charity which began its existence in the nineteenth-century East End. This was initially the work of William Booth (1829–1912), who began by establishing a Christian Mission in Whitechapel in 1865. Their mission was to undertake rescue work among the poorest of the poor, offering food, shelter and religious enthusiasm. The organisation's archives are held at William Booth College, Champion Park, Denmark Hill, London SE5 8BQ, telephone 020 7326 7800, email address: heritage@salvationarmy.org.

Other organisations include Toynbee Hall, Commercial Street, Whitechapel, founded by the Revd Samuel Barnett, Vicar of St Jude's in 1883, which was a scheme to involve idealistic students in educational and social work in the East End. It was probably the best-known institution of its type. THLHL&A holds numerous contemporary papers about

Statue of General Booth, Whitechapel Road (photo by the author).

its history, including Annual Reports, 1886–1993, journals 1936–9 and a centenary history. Then there is the Elizabeth Fry Probation Hostel, Shoreditch, (D/S/58) whose minutes, annual reports, log and report books, case books, 1846–1964, can be seen at HA. *The Siren* was the Stepney Rotary Club's magazine and copies from 1968–89 can be viewed at THLHL&A, as can the Oxford House magazine, 1909–36.

There were numerous almshouses in the East End, founded by businesses and individuals in order that certain aged individuals, often former employees or longstanding local residents of good character, should have a more comfortable old age than if they were forced to reside in a workhouse. In the East End these included Bancroft's, Drapers', East India Company's, George Green, Jewish, Norton Folgate, Skinners', Trinity House on White Cross Road. Shoreditch's Geffrye Almshouses are now a museum. Material which survives is variable. THLHL&A has papers for Sir John Jolles' almshouses (L/BSL/F/2/7) for 1903–40, about George Green Almshouse Trust (W/TUC/8/1–3) for 1955–74 and for the Nolgate Folgate almshouses (L/SMB/6/20), 1935–40.

Books

Interest both then and now in East End poverty has spawned numerous books and the primary sources fall into two main categories. There are books written by social reformers, such as Henry Mayhew and Charles Booth who wished to draw the attention of government and public to the plight of the poor. Then there are memoirs either by or about the poor by those who worked there, mostly written and published in the twentieth century. As with all such documents, some care needs to be taken. First, reformers have an agenda in their work – to show how miserable was the lot of those suffering from poverty – and so exaggeration would not therefore be unnatural. Those who knew poverty or knew of it were clearly writing from personal knowledge and it is possible that their first-hand experiences were not universal (and even their memories may not have been entirely accurate). These caveats apart, these books are often powerful statements and so should be read for the context they provide for our ancestors' lives. Several such memoirs are listed in the bibliography.

Chapter 4

CRIME AND VICE

Over time there have been some fearful and notorious murders committed in the East End: Jack the Ripper's murders in 1888, the Krays' crimes in the 1960s as well as the Ratcliff Highway Murders of 1811 and the Siege of Sidney Street in 1912. The internet, books, film, TV and even walking tours all serve to perpetuate the memory of the first two named. However, most crimes are relatively minor. Generally speaking, it is often easier to find out about criminal ancestors rather than the law abiding because records are created about the latter but not the former. Jennie Hawthorne noted that, in the 1920s, 'In the East End, crime of any sort, major or minor, was a constant topic of conversation as well as a way of life to take up or discard. The choice was not always in your own power' – she recalled a lad who would be beaten by his father if he came home without having stolen anything (*East End Memories*, 2005, p. 45). The classic tale of slum life and petty crime in Shoreditch in 1896 is well documented by Arthur Morrison in *A Child of the Jago*.

Court Records

There were a number of relevant courts which dealt with a variety of offences and there were no hard and fast rules as to which court was involved, though the magistrates' court would not be the final arbiter in capital offences.

From the sixteenth century to 1888 the Middlesex Quarter Sessions dealt with many crimes committed in the East End (and throughout the pre-1889 county of Middlesex). They dealt with thefts, assaults, political and religious offences, witchcraft, crimes against animals and much more. They could hand out sentences ranging from fines to hanging.

Fortunately for the family historian, as part of the great enthusiasm for calendaring records at the end of the nineteenth century, the Middlesex Quarter Sessions records were transcribed and published in 1886–1905 in six volumes, covering the years 1549–1709, with a second series of three volumes for 1612–16 published in 1935–7. They are arranged chronologically and give date, brief details of defendant/s, victim/s, offence and sentence, if any. Even more usefully, there are indexes by person, place and offence, so it is a relatively easy matter to ascertain if an ancestor was involved in crime and to what extent.

An example taken from the second series is as follows:

> 12 June, 12 James I (ad 1614)
>   John Brookes of Stepney, goldsmith, for stealing a petticoat worth 23s, a hat worth 22s, a hat lined with taffety worth 15s, 3 ruffs worth 35s, a safeguard worth 8s and an apron worth 18d from George Browne at the same.
>   Guilty, no goods, seeks the book, reads to be branded, but remanded to prison without bail.

The reference 'seeks the book' means that John Brookes pleaded 'Benefit of Clergy' which was a device used up to the early nineteenth century where a literate defendant, if he could prove he was able to read from the Bible, would have their sentence reduced, usually escaping the death penalty. This method of escape could only be used once, however, which is why they were branded on the thumb. Not all of the Quarter Session archives were transcribed. Those that are not (1710–1889) are held at the LMA.

This court was replaced by the London Court of Sessions in the new county of London, from 1889, which was formed from parts of Middlesex, Kent and Surrey. The main series of records produced by the court are court registers. These are held at the LMA, reference LJ/SR/001–697 and cover 1889–1945. The court sat twice a year until 1915, then quarterly. Court hearings for cases north of the Thames, thus all those from the East End, were held at Clerkenwell Sessions House, until 1919. Thereafter they were held at the same building as those for the south of the Thames, at Newington Sessions House. The court was

Shoreditch stocks (photo taken by Paul Howard Lang, 2017).

renamed the Inner London Sessions in 1946 and the court records are in the series ILS/B/13/001–276 for 1946–71.

An example of one of the records from LJ/SR/435, which covers a case from 1907:

> Nellie Cartwright was this day charged for that she on the 26th of May 1907 at Limehouse ... did feloniously receive one purse of the value of one shilling and the sum of £2 2 8 the goods and moneys of one Too Tack Ching well knowing the same to have been lately feloniously stolen from the person of the said Too Tack Ching ... bound by her mother's recognisance in the sum of £5 conditioned that she be to appear at this court for judgement and sentence ...

Dealing with lesser and more localised offences were the magistrates' courts. In our district there were the Thames Court, dealing with most of the East End, and the Old Street Magistrates' Court (sometimes and erroneously referred to as a police court) in Shoreditch was introduced in 1792 as one of seven magistrates' courts in London to deal with 'petty' offences. These included being drunk and disorderly, using insulting words and behaviour, prostitution, cruelty to horses, theft, motoring offences (in the twentieth century), failure to pay rates and many others. They also dealt with domestic matters, such as bastardy, claims for maintenance and adultery. Serious offences, such as murder, were often first heard at this court before being passed upwards, perhaps to the Old Bailey. Hearings were presided by a justice of the peace and there was no jury. Sentences were either custodial (up to six months in prison) or a fine.

The registers each cover about three months of a year. They are organised chronologically, and give the date of the court hearing, the name of the defendant, the offence they were accused of, the name of the witness, the verdict and the sentence. There are no indexes to names, so it can be quite a search unless an approximate date of the court hearing is known.

The Thames Court was located in Arbour Court, Stepney, from 1842, then at Charles Street in 1922, Aylward Street in 1937 and at the site of the former juvenile court on Bow Road from 1990. The Old Street Court was at Worship Street from 1792, then at Old Street from 1906.

The records are held at the LMA and are closed for 30 years. Those for the Thames Court cover 1804–1990 and comprise 1,124 volumes. They are as follows:

1. Court 1 part 1 registers, 1881–1971 PS/TH/A/01/001–478
2. Court 1 part 2 registers, 1884–1971 PS/TH/A/02/001–326

3. Court 2 registers, 1934–57 PS/TH/A/03/001–002
4. Petty Sessions registers, 1942–72 PS/TH/A/08/001–022

Those for the Old Street Court cover 1905–90 and comprise 515 volumes.

1. Court 1 part 1 registers, 1905–68 PS/OLD/A/01/001–245
2. Court 1 part 2 registers, 1905–68 PS/OLD/A/02/001–179
3. Court 2 registers, 1954–68 PS/OLD/A/03/001–004
4. Juvenile Court registers, 1959–63 PS/OLD/A/08/001–002
5. Married Women's Act, 1915–73, PS/OLD/B/01/001–041
6. Married Women's Act (Assaults), 1907–58, PS/OLD/B/02/001
7. Married Women's Act (Adultery: husbands), 1948–73, PS/OLD/B/03/001–004
8. Married Women's Act (Adultery: wives), 1950–71, PS/OLD/B/04/001

An example of the information to be gleaned from the Old Street Court Register reference PS/OLD/A1/005 is as follows, for 2 July 1907:

> Simon Glassoff charged with indecent assault, committed to the North London Sessions Court for trial.
>
> Ellen Enon, Rose Chatworthy, Alice Louisa Franklin, stealing and receiving 41 yards of silk, value £5 10 0 remanded until 3 July when committed to the North London Sessions.

Old Street Magistrates' Court (collection of John Coulter).

Alfred Thompson, loitering in a public place for purpose of betting, sentenced to a fine of £20 or two months in gaol.

Alfred Sharpe, unlawful possession of 5 ¼ ounces of scrap silver. Remanded until 9 July when given the option of a fine of 40s or a month in prison.

Walter Besant once wrote,

> I was once in a London police court looking on at the day's cases which were brought up one after the other before the magistrate. The drunk and disorderly came first; these were soon dismissed, indeed there is a terrible monotony about them, the reporters do not take the trouble even to listen or to make a note of them unless the prisoner is a man of some note.

Crown and Magistrates' Courts

In 1971 there was a dramatic revolution in the administration of justice in England and Wales in order to increase its efficiency. Gone were the quarter sessions and assizes and in came the magistrates' courts and Crown Courts, which replaced the two previous courts. Crown Courts deal with a minority of cases, the most serious, and the records are closed for 30 years. Those open to inspection are to be found at TNA (at J81–2) and can be searched for on their catalogue by name of defendant. Trial transcripts do not exist, but indictments papers and other records do. Records of magistrates' courts survive, if at all, at the court in question, to whom application for access should be made. The magistrates' court covering the East End was/is the Thames Magistrates' Court, 58 Bow Road, London E3 4DJ (tel. 020 8271 1530, email: londoneastmc@hmcts.gsi.gov.uk).

Finally there was the Old Bailey, or the Central Criminal Court, which dealt with offences throughout London and Middlesex. Although it is known as the place where murder and other high-profile cases are heard, it had a number of courts and these dealt with a great range of offences, just as the quarter sessions did. The level of detail found in these records is far more than in the quarter sessions or magistrates' courts, and the trials for 1678–1913 can be viewed on www.oldbaileyonline. They can be searched by name of defendant, victim or witness. Here is an example of a trial on 14 January 1764:

Thomas Bryan, was indicted, for stealing one wether sheep, val. 18s, the property of Simon Hillatt, Dec. 23.

Philip Gascoyne. I live at Poplar. I was in my garden about 7 o'clock at night, on the 23rd of Dec. I saw Mr Hillatt's sheep running about the field, which is near my garden; I went and saw the prisoner standing against the fence, and a sheep between his legs: Mr Floy was with me; I said, what is that man doing? He ran away directly, there was only a ditch between us, we pursued, and in about half a mile overtook him; we took him to Mr Rogers's, who looks after the marshes, and left him there, and went to the sheep; it was lying in the skin, which was taken off, and the head was in the ditch. Mr Hillatt swore to the sheep: he had taken the sheep out of Mr Hillatt's ground into a field next to it.

Mr Floy confirmed the account given.

Simon Hillatt. I am a butcher. Mr Rogers came to me the day before Christmas day, and told me what had happened; I went to his house the next day, and found the skin to be a skin of one of my sheep; I took that and the sheep home, and took the prisoner before the justice; there he said he was drove to it by necessity; that he had a man with him who told him, if he would go along with him he would shew him where he should have mutton enough: that they went to my field and catched one and killed it.

Q. What was the sheep worth?
Hillatt. It cost me 18s. I lost very little by it.
Q. to Gascoyne. Did you see any body with the prisoner?
Gascoyne. No, I did not.
Floy answered the same.
Prisoner's Defence.

I was coming from Deptford, crossing the river there is a foot way going to Poplar; I saw a man in the field, I asked him if that was the way to Poplar; when I was at a gate the man made away, I staid there about a quarter of an hour, then these 2 men came to me, I went from the place; and they catched me.

Guilty. Death. Recommended for mercy.

Police Records

London has been policed by the Metropolitan Police since 1829; the city being divided into divisions based on geography. Division H covered the East End. Most surviving police records concern police personnel, premises, equipment and policy. However, the records for serious crimes often do survive and are located at TNA in series MEPO2 and 3. These can be found by searching TNA's database by name of victim or perpetrator. Not all survive and even where they do, case files can have been seriously weeded.

There are summaries to murders and manslaughters in London for 1891–1958 in files MEPO20/1–5. That for a killing in Whitechapel is as follows:

> Wilful Murder of Frances Cole 13th Feby 1891 H Divn.
>
> At 2.15 am 13th February 1891 PC 240 Thompson was passing through Swallow Gardens, Royal Mint Street, Whitechapel, when he found the deceased lying in the roadway with her throat cut. The officer raised an alarm, and as soon as assistance arrived, sent for Dr Oxley of Dock Street who attended and pronounced life extinct. The body was conveyed to the Whitechapel Mortuary and was subsequently identified as that of Frances Cole, a Prostitute. It was ascertained that Sadler was the last person seen in the company of the deceased on 13th February and charged with wilful murder but was discharged by the magistrate in consequence of the prosecution having been withdrawn. A verdict of 'wilful murder against some person or persons unknown' was returned by the Coroners Jury.

The files usually include the report by the senior investigating officer, usually a chief inspector, which will highlight the key features of the case. There may also be witness statements and reports by others in the investigation team. There may be plans and photographs (often quite grim). They only exist for serious crimes, such as manslaughter, murder and treason, however. Some case files are still closed to researchers, such as the unsolved murder of Eileen Lockhart from Bow, murdered in 1948, but many are open, for example, that covering the mysterious death of Edith Emms in 1923, at MEPO3/852. They also cover other aspects of policing, such as police supervision of Wentworth Street Market, 1924–34 (MEPO3/2523), reports on prostitution in Stepney, 1957–64 (MEPO2/9715), correspondence relating to air raid precautions, 1939–42 (MEPO2/4928) and plans for married police quarters in Stepney in 1950 (MEPO9/241).

Old Bailey (collection of the author).

Coroners' Records

Those who have died outside hospital and in an unexpected manner are investigated. The majority of these are accidents and suicides (a criminal offence until 1961, of course) and only a minority are murders. Most coroners' papers do not survive (none do for parts of Whitechapel and St George's in the East for 1892–1940 and 1892–1956 respectively when they were within the Tower Liberty district) and those which do are closed for 75 years. Coroners' court records for the East End are held at the LMA. However, confusingly, different courts dealt with different parts of the East End at different dates. Until 1888, all were held by the Coroner for Middlesex Eastern District (MJ/SPC/E), but the creation of the LCC in the following year changed all that (until 1965 when all the East End fell under the jurisdiction of the Inner North London District (COR/IN)).

For Limehouse, Mile End, Poplar, Ratcliff, St George's (part), Shadwell and Stepney, they were part of the South Eastern District, 1888–92; Eastern District, 1892–1956; Southern District, 1956–65. Shoreditch was in the North Eastern District in 1888–1930; then the Eastern District, 1930–56 and then the Northern District. Whitechapel was partly in the South Eastern District, 1888–92; the Eastern District, 1892–1940; the Southern District, 1940–65. Stratford was in the North Eastern District, 1888–92 (COR/A); the Western District, 1892–4; the Eastern District, 1894–1912 (COR/ME) and then the Southern District, up to 1965 (COR/A/25–6).

It is often possible to locate more information about an inquest in the local press, who always report them (except during 1940–5 when they were not held on air raid victims, but were held on hanged murderers).

Newspapers

Crime is a staple ingredient of newspapers; from their point of view the gorier the better. Not all crimes are reported in the press. More serious crimes are there, of course, and can often be featured in a number of issues. Petty offences are often reported, though usually in less detail. National newspapers will often report murders and other major offences, but local newspapers will be useful for these and for lesser villainies. Fortunately, many national newspapers such as *The Times* and the *Daily Mirror* are digitised and can be searched (usually for a subscription fee, but often can be seen for free at places such as the British Library and the LMA).

An example of a newspaper report of a crime which hit the national press comes from *The Times* of 28 September 1923:

ASSAULT ON POLICE INSPECTOR

MAGISTRATE AND POPLAR DISTURBANCES

Arising out of the disturbances at the Poplar Board of Guardians Offices on Wednesday night, George Jones, 40, was charged at Thames Police [sic] Court yesterday with assaulting an inspector of police.

The inspector stated that the police were called to eject a number of men from the offices. The prisoner was coming out. On reaching the door, he said, 'Come on boys, we will give them something'. He then made a running kick at the witness, but the witness warded it off with his hand, which was injured. At the same time, the prisoner struck the witness on the side of his face, with his fist, causing a tooth to cut his cheek. At the police station, the prisoner said, 'I did it quite unintentionally. I am sorry. I wish I had never gone near the place, but at the same time, you know we don't recognise the English law'.

Scots Guards at the Siege of Sidney Street, 1912 (collection of John Coulter).

The witness added that there was great disorder, and that stones and tiles were thrown by the men.

The prisoner now declared that he had no sympathy with the men who made the disturbance, and only went to the hall to see his daughter, who had called there.

The MAGISTRATE remarked that one could not help having some pity for men like the prisoner. 'You are' he said 'made to believe that you are the victims of the social order. The whole world is suffering the terrible sequel of the war, and the thing that fills me with the burning indignation is that the men who live by inflaming your passions and put you in the position that you are in today, keep a whole hide and their personal freedom. Do you really think you are free to kick police officers and imprison citizens without restraint?'

In imposing a sentence of four weeks imprisonment, the magistrate said 'If this sort of thing goes on, instead of four weeks, I shall make the sentence six months hard labour'.

Local newspapers are often available at the relevant local history library or at the British Library Newspaper Room but will have to be ordered in advance in the latter case. Currently editions of the *East London Observer* for 1857–79 can be searched on the British Newspaper Archive site. One column of crime news reads as follows, from 1 July 1865:

PETTY THEFTS

At the Thames Police Court, John Harvey, aged 20, was charged with stealing a shilling from the till of Marshall Loader, his master.

The prosecutor is a pork butcher, and an extensive dealer in sausages, polonnies, saveloys and other delicacies, in Bedford Place, Commercial Road. Harvey had been long suspected of robbing the till, and he was watched, and was seen by a fellow shopman, named Joseph Lonhan, to put his hand into the till most deliberately, take a shilling out, and put it in his pocket. Lonhan told the 'governor' of the theft, and the prisoner was given into custody. A pound's worth of silver was found upon him, and in his box, two receipts of a post office savings bank for 8L 5s. The prisoner urged in defence the savings were honestly obtained, and that he was in receipt of 14 s a week from Mr Loader for 9 months, besides board and lodging. He denied the robbery.

The prisoner was committed for trial.

Sophie Field, aged 28, was charged with stealing a purse containing 35s from a sailor named Robert Nelson.

The sailor had been taking a cruise in the neighbourhood of Whitechapel, and he was staggering along Back Church lane, when the prisoner, one of the numerous land sharks in that quarter, marked him as her prey, and she very coolly took a purse containing 35s. worth of silver from his pocket and transferred it to her own. The robbery was observed by William Grayburn, a cigar maker of 29 Gloucester Buildings, New Road, St. George in the East, who immediately gave her into custody. The sailor, who said he was more than three sheets in the wind, had no recollection of the affair – only he misses his money.

Mr Partridge asked the prisoner if she would be tried by him, or prefer going to the sessions for trial.

Prisoner: I am innocent.

Mr Partridge: Then I shall commit you to trial.

Prisoner: Try me here, settle it at once, your worship.

Mr Partridge: I can't try you here if you say you are innocent.

Then I will plead guilty.

Mr Partridge: Don't do that if you are innocent. I don't wish you to plead guilty.

Prisoner: I am guilty, I plead guilty.

Mr Partridge: No doubt you are guilty. I sentence you to six weeks imprisonment and hard labour.

Court records, apart from those of the Old Bailey, can often be very sparse in information that they provide.

Another useful newspaper for those with criminal ancestors is the *Police Gazette*. This is a newspaper circulated within the police themselves and details people wanted by the police. Descriptions of people wanted are provided and this can be the only physical description of the person. The newspaper can be searched on Ancestry.co.uk for the years 1812–1902 and 1921–7. It is closed for 75 years, though application to Scotland Yard may allow access to microfilm copies at the British Library Newspaper Library.

Memoirs

Crime, as has already been noted, is a topic of great interest to most people. Those involved in crime have been known to pen their memoirs, whether as police officers, lawyers, doctors or as criminals. These can provide insights, not only into crime and its detection (or not as the case may be), but also the working lives of those involved, and to the social milieu in which they operated. The Kray brothers were certainly 'celebrity criminals' and both wrote their memoirs which detail their own interpretations of their lives and actions, justifying themselves and their deeds. How accurate they are is another question, of course. Reg Kray also wrote *Villains we have Known* in 1993 and this includes brief portraits of nearly 80 criminals such as Big Jimmy Kensit from Shoreditch, a street fighter and boxer, and Willie and Charlie Malone from Stepney, former dockers turned pugilists. As mentioned in chapter 2, there are several memoirs of police officers who served in the East End in the previous two centuries.

Other Sources

Two online sources on Ancestry.co.uk which will be of use for criminals are the Middlesex Transportation Contracts from 1682–1787 and transportation listings for 1787–1868, when convicts could be sent to the American colonies and from 1787 to Australia. These records supply the name of the convict, that of the vessel sailed in to the American colonies/Australia, depending on date, date of conviction, date of voyage, place of conviction and colony sent to. For the Australia-bound convicts, the term of transportation in years is also provided. There are additional searchable sources on the same website for those despatched 'Down Under' as the level of bureaucracy was higher than in previous times.

Then there are the London Criminal Registers, 1791–1892, taken from Home Office files at TNA. These can also be seen at Ancestry.co.uk and can be searched by name. They list prisoner, place and date of detention prior to trial, date and result of trial, and if applicable, date of execution or transportation. There will be personal details of the prisoner to enable identification: age, height, colour of eyes and hair, complexion, occupation and birthplace. For more recent malefactors, at TNA are printed calendars of London wrongdoers in sequence CRIM9, covering 1855–1949. They are, however, closed for 75 years, so at time of writing those for 1942–9 are inaccessible. They are arranged by county and give similar information to the earlier registers, with the additions of level of literacy and further details of the crime committed.

Prison records for some London prisons are held at the LMA, such as those for Wandsworth, Wormwood and Holloway, but not Brixton or

Pentonville, and can be viewed, but are not indexed by name. Arranged in chronological order, they list the date of imprisonment and the date of departure; either to freedom or to another gaol (possibly outside London), as well as name, level of education and religious denomination. Bear in mind that the sentence issued at the end of the trial is not the one necessarily served; execution was frequently commuted to transportation or gaol or Broadmoor (records held at Berkshire Record Office but closed for 100 years after the death of the patient) and prisoners rarely serve the full sentence given but mostly receive remission due to good behaviour. These records are now closed for 75 years for data protection reasons.

On a lesser note, those who did not pay their rates when requested were often recorded in council records. Rate Summons for Shoreditch for 1907–48 (S/FRS/1-6) show those ratepayers who did not to pay up on time and can be seen at HA.

Finally, if your ancestors had the dubious fortune to be mixed up with any of the East End's most notorious crimes, then it would be advisable to consult some of the vast literature on these cases. There are several books on the Krays, the Ratcliff Highway Murders and the siege of Sidney Street. Yet far outstripping these foul deeds is the mini-industry set up in the aftermath of Jack the Ripper. A lot of research has been undertaken on the unfortunate women who fell prey to the Ripper's knife and so we know a great deal about Mary Ann Nichols, Annie Chapman, Elizabeth Stride, Catherine Eddowes, and Mary Jane Kelly as well as a few others who may also have been victims in the Autumn of Terror and beyond. These books are very variable in quality and detail however, for most focus on 'solving' the mystery, but with over a hundred people, often very well-known personalities of the time, being variously named, we can be certain that most, if not all, are incorrect. They tend to bend and stretch evidence which is tenuous at best and are big on theory. Several books can be recommended, because they stick to known facts and do not try and impose a suspect on the reader. These include Philip Sugden's *The Complete Jack the Ripper* (2004) and Donald Rumbelow's *Jack the Ripper* (2006). *The Ultimate Jack the Ripper Source Book*, edited by Stewart Evans and Keith Skinner in 2000, reproduces all the key primary documents in the case from myriad sources and so is also recommended.

Chapter 5

WAR AND RIOT

The East End, by dint of its location, was particularly vulnerable to aerial bombardment during both world wars (1914–18 and 1939–45). By being at the east of London it was closer for German zeppelins and aircraft than other parts of the capital. Secondly its proximity to the docks also made it vulnerable, as the docks and warehouses were crucial to Britain's war effort and so prime targets. Much of the East End was destroyed and damaged in the Second World War by bombing. Many of its residents were killed or wounded. During the Second World War, the statistics for Stepney, Poplar and Bethnal Green were as follows: deaths 2,221, injured 7,472, houses destroyed 46,482, houses damaged 47,574. There are numerous sources for Eastenders whose lives were affected by the world wars.

Before the world wars, there was a volunteer regiment recruited and serving in the district. This was the Tower Hamlets Militia. Its origins lay in the seventeenth century and it continued in existence until the nineteenth. The militia was often summoned to suppress riots and keep the peace. There are a number of muster rolls in existence and these are to be found at TNA. For 1644, see SP28/121A; for enrolment lists and pay lists for 1817–53, see WO68/432 and 437 respectively; returns for the men for 1805–16 are at WO13/2561–2. East End newspapers also refer to these men, especially to their regular social and sporting occasions.

Servicemen

Many East Enders joined the regular forces. Poverty is often an effective recruiting sergeant and so the young men of the East End were more susceptible than most to the recruiting sergeant's blandishments. Jennifer

Worth was told by an old man how he joined the Scots Guards in the late nineteenth century as a lad of 15 (he said he was 17). The lad was seen by a recruiter and given a good meal (he had had nothing for breakfast) and told of the advantages of an army life. He joined up.

Millions of Britons joined the uniformed services during the world wars. In 1914–15 the ranks were filled by volunteers but in 1916–18 and 1939–45 conscription was introduced to supply the manpower needed. Although only men served on the front line, many women served in supporting roles throughout the three fighting services. There have been numerous books about tracing service ancestors so what follows here is but a brief summary.

For First World War ancestors, the first port of call should be Ancestry. co.uk to check service records, and failing that, as many records do not survive, pension records on the same site (again, not all survive). These tell the name, address, occupation and next of kin. They state date of enlistment and expiry of service, unit/s/ship/s served in. References to promotions, postings overseas, disciplinary offences and wounds/ death appear. The medal records database on Ancestry.co.uk should also

War memorial at Macey Street, Bethnal Green (photo by the author).

be checked as virtually all of these survive, but the information there is limited to name, rank and unit/s served in as well as details of medals gained; often only the British Medal, the Victory Medal and for those serving from 1914, the 1914 Star. Medals for gallantry are limited.

For Second World War ancestors, contact should be made to the appropriate records centre of the Ministry of Defence for service records of individuals are still housed there. They tend to be more copious than those created in the Great War and almost all survive. Medical records are only available to next of kin.

Some records are common to both wars. Deaths in service were more common in the First World War, and both they and deaths in the later war can be found on the Commonwealth War Graves Commission website, which can be searched by name. These records show name, rank, unit, age on death and location of grave. Records for officers mostly survive and can be viewed at TNA; Army, Navy and RFC/RAF lists were produced on a monthly basis during wartime and can help trace an officer's career. These can be viewed at the TNA's library. Court martial records are available to view at TNA; some are searchable on the TNA's website Discovery but most are not.

Local sources should also be examined. First, the local newspapers published material about servicemen, though there is more to be found for the earlier conflict. Newspapers often listed men who had volunteered, giving name, address and unit enlisted in; after conscription in 1916, often lists of men wanted were published, giving names and addresses (no such listings appear for the Second World War). Then if a man is killed, wounded, taken prisoner or decorated for gallantry, there should be a paragraph or two about them and possibly a photograph, too. Letters from soldiers serving abroad were often published, but there will be no reference to any operational details.

As an example, we'll take an article published in the *East London Observer* of 30 January 1915:

> STEPNEY LIBRARIAN KILLED IN ACTION
>
> News has been received with much regret of the first death in action among the members of the Stepney Library staff, who enlisted for the war. Mr Fred Budgen left the staff of the Stepney Library three years ago to join the army. He went out to India, first of all, and in due course was sent from there direct to the Front. There he was killed in action on November 27th. The following letter from the chaplain of the 7th Dragoon Guards to the deceased's brother relates the sad circumstances.

'Your brother was killed whilst the regiment was in the trenches by being hit in the head by a shrapnel bullet. He never, I am told, regained consciousness, although he was alive when he reached the hospital. Owing to the censorship, I am unable to tell you where he was buried … You will be glad to know that a decent burial was given him, a clergyman officiating … All his comrades were present. We have lost in him a fine and promising comrade and soldier.
Yours truly,
Tom A. Cairnes, captain'

Mr Fred Budgen was only 22 years of age, but he had earned the professional respect of his colleagues whilst he was in Stepney as he did when serving in the Army.

War Memorials and rolls of honour were often produced by the borough, churches, schools, workplaces and clubs in the years following the end of the wars to mark the service of their members who had fought. These may be restricted to those who were killed, but some include those who were not. Some include rank, unit and decorations, but by no means all.

Commonwealth War Graves Commission

The Commission has compiled a vast register of those civilians and servicemen killed in First and Second World Wars. It was arranged by borough and then alphabetically by name. Information given is name, age, occupation, address, date and place of death. It can be accessed for free at www.cwgc.com. Please note that there were no inquests on those killed by bombing during the War and so it is pointless to search through the coroners' records hoping to find them. Those injured, who greatly exceed those killed, are harder to find information about, but hospital records should be checked (see chapter 9).

Newspapers

This is a less useful source than ordinarily because paper was rationed and so newspapers had far fewer pages than in peacetime and because newspaper editors were reluctant to print anything which might assist the enemy. Therefore the names of buildings/streets destroyed or damaged would not be mentioned. However, the names of those killed were often reported, sometimes in the Births, Marriages and Deaths and obituaries sections.

Apart from the very real risk to life, limb and property caused by the bombing, global conflict had other impacts on the population and some of these are reflected in the local press. These do not always mention individuals by name but give an indication of activity occurring locally. The impact of air raids in the First World War were described in the local press. On 23 June 1917 the *East London Observer* reported:

> The child victims of the Air Raid
> Wednesday's Ceremony
> Amid most impressive and affecting scenes, the child victims of the East End school bombed last week were carried to their last resting place, the East London Cemetery, on Wednesday … The service at Poplar Parish Church was the most stirring for its simplicity. The hymns were those known and loved by every child, 'There's a Friend for little children', 'Loving Shepherd of thy sheep' and 'O God our help in ages past' and the psalm was the 23rd, the first poem, in many cases, which the infants at school learn by heart. The Bishop of London was assisted, and the service by the bishop of Stepney and the Rev. O.S. Lawrie, Rector of Poplar, conveyed to the mourners the following message from the King.

There were also reports about the visit of Queen Mary to the Poplar Hospital, touring the wards to speak to the survivors of the air raid, and to give them gifts. There was also an editorial which was critical of the government for failing to properly defend the capital's people from the deadly air raids, with a lack of warnings and a lack of an adequate defence thereafter.

Newspapers in 1914–15 often reported appeals to men to volunteer for the armed forces. This could take the form of adverts. But it also covers public events, such as concerts, talks and recruiting drives, all designed with the same objective. If you know when your ancestor volunteered for service (by checking his enlistment papers), then checking newspapers just before his date of enlistment you may well find reports of one of these events. For 1916–18 conscription was imposed and then the newspapers were full of reports of local men who went before the tribunals to explain why they should not be called up to fight for their country. Contrary to popular opinion, the majority who were resistant to war service were not conscientious objectors who were motivated by religion, politics or morality but men who had business or family reasons why they could not join – often they were the sole family breadwinner or were the key member of a business or had a vulnerable family member. These

Spitalfields war memorial (photo by the author).

tribunals might give details of the family/business of your ancestor. Usually, though, they were given a set time to put their affairs in order before being called up.

The heroism and tragedy of war was also reflected in the press in the Second World War. The *East London Advertiser* of 15 February 1941 ran the following story:

> BOW MAN WINS BAR TO DFM
> Helped to destroy Six Enemy Planes
> **Clerk who became Air Gunner**
> A Bow clerk who became an air gunner in the RAF, and who won the DFM in June of last year, has now won a further honour, having gained a bar to the DFM.
>
> He is Sergt. F.J. Baker, who was born in Bow in 1918, and his father is still a resident there. Before the war, Sergt. Baker was a clerk, in 1939 he entered in the RAF, as a wireless operator and air gunner under training.
>
> **Both honoured**
> In June last year he was an air gunner of a machine piloted by Flt. Sergt. E.R. Thorn, and took part in the destruction of six enemy aircraft. For this, both Sergt. Thorn and Sergt. Baker was awarded the DFM.
>
> Now both their names appear in the list of airmen who have received the bar to the DFM for further gallantry. They belong to the 264 Squadron.

The end of both wars saw jubilation and relief on the part of the civil population and this was both organised and also spontaneous. These events in the streets and elsewhere were recorded in the local press – often with pictures in 1945.

Memoirs, letters and diaries provide personal responses to the war. At THLHL&A are the memoirs of evacuee Kitty Wintrub (LC7849) and extracts from the letters of Rachel Reckitt from Stepney (L9381). The latter covering 1940–1 largely focus on the human problems caused by the bombing, rather than the damage per se. For instance, she records her annoyance at West Enders 'getting an evening's amusement sight seeing in the East End shelters. I should hardly cause it amusement'. Exasperation at the inactivity of local officials was another there: 'The arrangements in Stepney are hopelessly inadequate. I can't imagine what the authorities have been doing as they must have foreseen all this; after all it was obvious that the Thameside area would get it worst'. It was not all doom and gloom as she also recalled, 'The King came down yesterday, which cheered people up and either he or Churchill came yesterday, which cheered people up too'.

Bomb Damage Maps

A bomb census was begun in London and elsewhere in September 1940 to create a complete picture of bomb damage. Information about bombs dropped was collected and sent to the Ministry of Home Security, and collated on standard forms. The information given was: date and time of bomb falling, type and size of bomb, whether it exploded or not, description of damage and size of crater and information on air raid warnings given. It is found at TNA in series HO198. There is often a sketch map appended. This information in HO198 is sub-divided thus, 1–73 covering bombs dropped from aircraft, 74–102 for the V1 flying rockets and 103–9 the V2 rockets. The forms are then divided by date and Civil Defence Regions, with London being Region 5, which is further sub-divided by (pre-1965) borough. Sometimes incidents are further detailed and these accounts can be found in HO192 and searched by keyword. Plans and photographs are often included here.

Maps of boroughs were made which show where bombs dropped, usually with a date and the type of bomb. For London, there are the Bomb Census maps at TNA, in series HO193, with 1–11, 15–40 and 84–7 covering those of aircraft, 48–50 for V1 and V2 rockets.

The LCC made its own bomb damage maps. These were published, *The London County Council Bomb Damage Maps, 1939–1945*, with an introduction by Robert Woolven in 2005 (and again in 2015 by the LMA/Thames & Hudson). The Imperial War Museum has a large collection of written and oral reminiscences of civilians and civil defence workers as well as relevant photographs.

Ordnance survey maps produced in the 1950s should not be overlooked for they will note gaps where buildings once stood and indicate ruined buildings.

The website www.bombsight.org covers London from 1940–1, showing locations of bombs together with associated material, such as photographs and testimonies of witnesses.

Council Archives

During the Second World War councils were responsible for civil defence. This meant that they had to form a temporary committee of councillors to discuss policy and implementation and to appoint paid officials to work full time to ameliorate the effect that aerial bombing would have on the civil population. THLHL&A holds civil defence archives for the boroughs of Bethnal Green, Poplar and Stepney.

For Bethnal Green there are the civil defence committee minutes books covering September 1939–September 1940 (L/BGM/A/18/1/2–4) and the General Emergency Committee Minutes for 1939–46 (L/BGM/A/17/1/1–18). For Stepney in this period, see L/SMB/A/20. Poplar's archives are rather better, with the entirety of the Second World War being covered (L/PMB/A/14/2–9). Shoreditch's civil defence records from 1936–53 are to be found at HA. The council minutes for the meetings of all of the council exist in published format and, as they are well indexed, are another useful source for local and family history for the East End in the Second World War.

Much of the information in the minutes shows how the committee dealt with the issues arising from the bombing. These included rehousing the homeless, repairing those properties which were not damaged beyond repair. There were lists of expenditure, often listing the different bids by contractors and showing which was chosen (usually the cheapest) and requisitions of empty houses. Information was given about the air raid shelters in the borough, many of which were provided by employers in the district, noting type of shelter, location and accommodation offered therein. For example, W. Pross & Son had a shelter at their premises on 94 Fairfield Road, which was a concrete underground shelter which could safeguard 60 people.

There was information about procedures, such as the burial of the dead caused by air raids. The borough would pay for the burials of those families who could not afford them. However, the committee gave a grant of £7 10s for the burial of those who had died whilst on civil defence duties. References to the cumulative damage in the borough are made; by 2 February 1941, 16,800 buildings had been damaged, though 12,942 could be repaired. A total of 51 builders were employed to undertake this work.

The Poplar minute book describes the brave action of Mr E H Smith, their chief air raid warden, during the Blitz in December 1940, which won him the George Cross. There was a fire at Bow church made more potentially dangerous by a gas flare being nearby:

> Mr Smith entered the bombed premises and got through to the destroyed portion. Here he climbed over the loose debris, with the roof and parts of the floor hanging over him. He could not reach the gas piping which had a flame of 10 to 15 feet at the end of it, so with a hook he pulled this down and called for wet cloths. With a small piece of cloth he endeavoured to put the flame out with his hands, and finally with a wet coat and blanket he succeeded in smothering the gas.

These minute books are particularly interesting if your ancestor was involved in civil defence as many civilians were. The Poplar Minute Book for 1940–1 notes that on 26 April 1941, Mr S Gidlowe was no longer the borough's surveyor as from 12 March 1941 for he had been called up for military service. It also notes three joiners. Mr D A Ford replaced Gidlowe as surveyor as from 17 March 1941. He was 28 years old and would receive an annual salary of £300 plus bonuses. Mr A J Hill, aged 62, was employed from 5 April 1941 for £5 9s 2d per week. Finally there was Mr E H Smith, aged 52, employed as clerk for war damage on 24 April 1941 on £3 11s 1d per week. There was a monthly magazine of the Stepney ARP Service for 1939–40, held at THLHL&A. Civil defence workers who were decorated for gallantry can be found among the Civil Defence Gallantry Medals, 1940–9, on Ancestry.co.uk.

The impact of the bombing is rather better recorded by these three councils. There are 85 air raid damage files for Bethnal Green from August 1940 to February 1945 (L/BGM/B/11/1–85). The infamous Bethnal Green shelter disaster of 1943, the worst of its kind in the country, is dealt with by an Enquiry (L/BGM/D/2/11). For Poplar there are casualty lists, 1940–5 (L/PMB/B/5/3) and listings of air raid incidents for the same years (L/PMB/B/5/4). Shoreditch's civilian fatalities are listed in HA at S/R/2/3.

Bethnal Green Council carefully recorded bombs which dropped on the borough. Report sheets were completed by air raid staff for each 'incident' that they were called out for, once they had been there. Information recorded there included date and time of the report, location, type of bomb/s fallen, emergency services there, damage to water mains, whether there was a fire, which roads were blocked, whether there had been any unexploded bombs and any casualties. One example from the night of 10 November 1940 tells the researcher that they were summoned at 21.35 to the junction of Bonner Road/St James' Avenue/Bandon Road. A high-explosive bomb had been dropped there and the damage to buildings had blocked the road from nine o'clock. There had, however, been no casualties and no fire.

Finally there are some photographs of Stepney during the war: an album showing civil defence employees from 1940–4 (P/MIS/173) and photograph albums for 1938–41 (L/SMB/D/4/12, 14). Many more photographs exist in THLHL&A's collections and reference to these can be found on the online catalogue.

One of the worst civilian tragedies in London on the evening of 3 March 1943, a year in which bombing was generally lighter than in the years to either side, occurred at Bethnal Green.

> Immediately the alert was sounded a large number of people left their houses in the utmost haste for shelter. A great many were running. Two cinemas at least in the near vicinity disgorged a large number of people and three omnibuses set down their passengers near to the shelter.

The crush of people rushing to shelter following the air raid siren led to 174 people losing their lives. A full enquiry resulted and the findings were published. They can be found in the book, *Tragedy at Bethnal Green, 1943*, republished in 1999.

Evacuation of children was a feature of life in London in 1939–45. Although it was not compulsory, many children were sent by train or bus to safety away from the impending aerial assault. The evacuation scheme was organised at county council level. Archives relating to evacuation are thus held at the LMA, and their online information sheets cover this topic. There are, however, no listings of evacuees. Reference to evacuees can be found in the school logbooks (discussed in more detail in chapter 9) and in the local press, which published stories of happy evacuees in the countryside. These rarely refer to individuals, however, but it is usually possible to ascertain what happened to pupils from particular schools. Many schools in the East End reopened as pupils drifted back home when

Bethnal Green underground disaster memorial (photo by the author).

the expected bombardment failed to materialise. Logbooks often refer to air raid precautions, drill and when lessons were interrupted due to raids. Medical Officer of Health Annual Reports (discussed in detail in chapter 9) also give information about school children during the world wars.

The logbook for Culloden Street School (held as a copy for 1940–7 at THLHL&A, L7888) is a good source of information for this East End school in the Second World War. In 1940 there are lists of children who were evacuated, with addresses and when they returned to school. For June 1944, with the onset of the V1 rocket, entries read:

> 16 June Air Raids
> Attendance am = 15 pm = 44 owing to air raids – Day spent in shelters
> 19 June
> Alert sounded 9.30 am all children to shelters. Raiders passed at 11.5. Attendance bad after all night alert.

In March 1945, the school was damaged by enemy action and a damage survey was carried out. Finally on 8 and 9 May the school was closed, due to 'Victory in Europe' celebrations.

Additional material about the East End during the Second World War, including photographs, oral testimonies and audio-visual material, can be found at the library of the Imperial War Museum.

Riot and Unrest

Civil disorder occasionally breaks out in most cities for social, economic, religious and political reasons. There have been a number of major disturbances in the East End. They occupy the attention of the media, the politicians, police and sometimes the army, as well as contemporary observers. Spitalfields was the scene of at least three major riots in the eighteenth century: in 1719, 1736 and 1768, all for economic reasons. These are covered in the State Papers Domestic series 35, 36 and 37 respectively and in the Secretary of State's Entry Books at SP44, with letters to and from the minister responsible for law and order (the equivalent office to the Home Secretary prior to 1782). These papers are available at TNA.

Mural of Cable Street battle (photo by Paul Lang).

Sir Robert Walpole's correspondence, published by William Coxe in 1798, deals with the 1736 rioting, which occurred over a number of nights and where it was concerned that there might be political undertones. He wrote:

> On Tuesday night evening they assembled again in greater bodies, and were, about seven a clock, thought to be above two thousand in number. They now grew more riotous; they attacked a publick house kept by an Irishman, where the Irish resorted and victualled, broke down all the doors and windows, and quite gutted the house. Another house of the same sort underwent the same fate.

Walpole then went on to report the methods used to control the situation and its causes. Records of the courts and trials, noted in chapter 4, provide information about those accused and their fates. Police archives are useful for more recent disturbances and at TNA can be seen files MEPO2/3060 and 3098 which consist of letters and reports about the Battle of Cable Street of 1936. The press also featured these riots, and though there was no East End press prior to the mid-nineteenth century, other newspapers covered them, such as *The Political State of Great Britain* (1711–40), *The Gentleman's Magazine* (1731–1868) and *The Annual Register* (1758 onwards). The *Derby Mercury* reported an aspect of the 1768 rioting thus:

> Friday last the several persons of the house where the weavers' work was said to be cut at the looms; this Day se'nnight by persons armed, mask'd, &c. underwent a long examination before Sir John Fielding at the police office at Bow Street, when it appeared, to the great satisfaction as well of many silk manufacturers as journeymen, who attended in the occasion, that the above works were wilfully destroyed by a Girl, who was at work upon them; viz by one Anne Winters, a journey woman to one Dilland, a weaver so that the public may rest assured, that there have been no outrage committed by the weavers since the commitment of William Evans to Newgate, nor does there appear at present any Dissatisfaction to subsist between the manufacturers and the journeymen in Spitalfields.

Much the same can be said about more recent disorders, such as the racial conflicts which turned nasty on the streets of Whitechapel and Spitalfields in the 1970s. Then, life was made hard for the newly arrived Pakistani and Bangladeshi residents by political extremists from elsewhere in London who attacked them and their property. One of the worst incidents was when Altab Ali was killed in 1978 on Adler Street by three teenagers (a park is now named after him). Memoirs of activists can give one side of the story and of the fight back, whilst letters in the local press give a variety of reactions, but any police archives at TNA are likely to be closed for some time to come. THLHL&A has an extensive coverage of racist attacks in its news cutting files.

Memorial Park, Whitechapel (photo by the author).

Chapter 6

RELIGIONS IN THE EAST END

Faith played a major role in most people's lives until the nineteenth century and in some cases, beyond. Simon Webb wrote that in the East End, 'Something which those under the age of fifty or so might find hard to grasp is the extent to which, in the 1960s, our lives were permeated and underpinned by religion'. Although in the sixteenth and seventeenth centuries and afterwards, the Anglican Church was dominant, there were a variety of other religious practices in the East End. From the seventeenth century these were other Christian denominations, not only reflecting native diversity in faith, but also that of peoples from other countries, notably France, Germany and Russia. There were also non-Christian faiths from Eastern Europe and beyond, notably Judaism from the seventeenth to the twentieth centuries and Islam from the later twentieth century. Although it is impossible to separate immigrants from their religions, this chapter will attempt to deal with purely religious matters whereas chapter 7 will deal with the secular sources for immigrants, old and new. The information found in http://www.ideastore.co.uk/local-history-resources-places-of-worship-guide is also recommended.

The Church of England

From the sixteenth to the early nineteenth century, England's government was largely overseen at local level by the parish, which was also the lowest level of ecclesiastical administration. The Church played a part in what were, from the nineteenth century onwards, secular matters, in both government and law. Thus it dealt with non-Anglicans as well as

Anglicans. There are at least two areas of prime importance for family historians.

Parish registers are the single most important source for the family historian for the sixteenth to the nineteenth century, for they list names of those married, being baptised and being buried, with dates of these events, and for baptism, usually the parents' names, too. Although churchgoing was not common in the East End by the late nineteenth century (less than 10 per cent being regular attendees), these ceremonies were frequent. James Mayne, curate in Bethnal Green from 1823 to 1842 claimed he performed 800 baptisms, 180 marriages and 670 burial services each year.

Most, if not all, of these parish records can be searched on Ancestry. co.uk: baptisms up to 1906, marriages up to 1921 and all burials. For registers following these dates you will need to visit the LMA and see the registers on microfilm (original records are not produced to avoid wear and tear). More recent registers are still held at the churches to whom enquiry should be made.

The information provided is as follows, with examples.

Baptisms

Up to 1812, name of child and of parents and date of baptism. On 1 May 1728 at the church of St Mary le Bow, George, son of James and Elizabeth Puller was baptised. After 1812, additional information is provided; father's occupation and the family address (usually inexact); might include date of birth. At Christ Church, Spitalfields, the baptism on 18 October 1840 of Alfred George, son of Thomas and Mary Ann Grayson was recorded. The father was a dyer and they lived at Flower and Dean Street (in Spitalfields).

Marriages

Up to 1754, names of both parties and date of marriage. For example, on 29 December 1700, at St Mary's church, Whitechapel, Marmaduke Billett of George Street, Stepney, and Elinor Ricketts of Whitechapel were wed. From 1754 additional information is recorded; age (might only state 'full age' which means 21 or over), marital status and occupation of both parties; their signatures, name and occupation of fathers of both parties, names of witnesses, who were often family members. On 25 October 1858 at St Peter's church, Mile End, William Bignell, a 33-year-old widower who was a tobacco pipe maker and Catherine Sechler, a 42-year-old widow, were wed. His father was William, a hairdresser and

Christ Church Spitalfields, 1815 (collection of Lindsay Siviter).

hers was Joseph Benton, a licensed victualler. Both the parties lived in Essex Street.

Burials

Up to 1812, name of individual buried, where known, and date of burial. On 2 December 1750, the burial register for St George in the East simply recorded that Sarah Shores, widow of Harris Court, was buried. After 1812, additionally age and address (often only parish last resided in) is noted. The burial register of Christ Church, Spitalfields, recorded that, on 13 February 1835, Philip Jones of Ross Lane, aged 22, was buried.

Additional information might be included at the clerk's whim – such as whether a child baptised was black, for example. Note that burial registers only exist for churches consecrated prior to the early nineteenth centuries.

Banns

From 1754, banns are read out in the church where the couple are to wed on three Sundays before the marriage is to take place in case anyone has any legal objections as to why the ceremony cannot take place. They provide the names of both parties, their marital status and the parish in which they dwell. An example is as follows, taken from the Banns of All Saints, Poplar. On 16, 23 and 30 October 1825 it was noted that 'Edward Long of this parish, widower & Sarah Blackbourne of the same, widow' had their banns read out on each occasion.

There are other registers listing important events in the spiritual life of those concerned. These are the Confirmation Registers. These list details of a person being confirmed into the church, arranged in chronological order. Unlike baptisms, marriages, banns and burials, most confirmation registers are not available online at Ancestry.co.uk; you will need to go to the LMA to see them on microfilm. The only church in the East End for which they are available is St Matthew's, Bethnal Green. They provide, in date order, the name of the person to be confirmed, their age and address, the date of the ceremony and of their first communion. For instance, at St Matthew's church in Bethnal Green, on 13 June 1897 Joseph Theophilus Parfit of 63 Cheshire Street, aged 63, was confirmed as a full member of the Church, thereafter able to take the holy communion of bread and wine, and did so for the first time on 27 June 1897.

Do remember that, although people in previous centuries were far more likely to attend church and to have their families pass through these major ceremonies (until 1689 non-attendance at the parish church was a punishable offence), many did not do so in the nineteenth century onwards, especially among the poorer classes. On the other hand, burials are an inescapable part of life and, until the building of the cemeteries in the nineteenth century, a burial service in church was hard to avoid.

Until 1837 parish registers are essential because there were no certificates of civil registration. After that date the two systems, religious and civil, ran in tandem. Parish registers capture much of the same information as civil registration certificates and to an extent they are a cheaper way of acquiring the same information. Many people, of course, and especially in the mid and late nineteenth century, did not have their births recorded by the civil authorities, especially among the poor.

Parish registers are also of great interest to the local historian. They can be used to investigate topics such as population growth, mortality, family sizes, occupational structure, migration, to name but a few.

The table shows the whereabouts of East End parish registers and other key parish archives which have been deposited in a number of record offices, where they can be viewed on microfilm. THLHL&A has many of these on microfilm, too; chiefly covering the years prior to 1837.

East End parish registers and archives

	Baptisms	Marriages	Burials	Other
All Hallows, Devons Road, Bromley by Bow	1875–1967	1875–1971		**Parish Magazines, 1927–91**
All Hallows, East India Dock Road, Poplar	1880–1940	1880–1929		Banns, 1929–47, **Parish Magazines, 1903–32**
All Saints, East India Dock Road	1728–2004	1733–2009	1813–1917	Banns, 1823–2001 Confirmations, 1991–2002, **Parish Magazines, 1900–56**

All Saints, Buxton Street, Mile End	1840–1951	1840–1951		Banns, 1895–1936
Christ Church, New North Road, Hoxton	1839–1944	1841–1953		Banns, 1939–45, Confirmations, 1913–39
Christ Church, Jamaica Street	1877–98	1878–1941		
Christ Church, Manchester Road, Isle of Dogs	1876–1979	1857–1991		Banns, 1857–1993, Confirmations, 1960–98
Christ Church, Spitalfields	1729–1961	1729–1998	1729–1859	Banns, 1761–1911, Confirmations, 1929–95
Christ Church, Watney Street	1842–1945	1842–1947		
Holy Trinity, Bletchley Street, Hoxton	1848–1936	1848–1943		Banns, 1848–1915
Holy Trinity, Morgan Road, Mile End	1841–1938	1841–1989		Banns, 1960–72, **Parish Magazines, 1949–64**
Holy Trinity, Old Nichol Street, Bethnal Green	1867–92	1889–1923		
St Agatha, Finsbury Avenue, Shoreditch	1871–1937			
St Anne, Hoxton Street	1870–1959	1870–1922		Banns, 1904–59
St Andrew's, Canal Road, Hoxton	1865–1944	1865–1946		Banns, 1933–41, Confirmations, 1930–44
St Andrew's, Viaduct Street, Bethnal Green	1843–1957	1843–1957		Banns, 1952–7, **Parish Magazines, 1916–38**

St Andrew's, Poplar	1900–49	1901–48		**Parish Magazines, 1893–1938**
St Anne's, Limehouse	1730–1955	1731–1968	1730–1897	Banns, 1911–75, **Parish Magazines, 1943–95**
St Anthony's, Globe Road, Stepney	1879–1933	1880–1936		
St Augustine's, Yorkton Street, Stepney	1879–1948	1880–1946		
St Barnabas, Grove Road, Bethnal Green	1870–2001	1871–1960		Banns, 1959–81
St Bartholomew's, Coventry Road, Bethnal Green	1844–1949	1844–1955	1844–1957	**Parish Magazines, 1966–7**
St Benet's, Mile End Road, Stepney	1931–40	1929–51		
St Dunstan's, Rectory Square, Stepney	1568–1937	1568–1941	1568–1856	Banns, 1732–1963, Confirmations, 1929–48, **Parish Magazines, 1973–2002**
St Faith's, Shandy Street, Stepney	1891–1945	1891–1940		
St Gabriel, Chrisp Street	1869-1947	1869-1947		Confirmations, 1937–42
St George in the East, Cannon Street Road	1729–1928	1729–1966	1729–1875	Banns, 1934–66, Confirmations, 1926–40

St James the Great, Bethnal Green Road, Bethnal Green	1844–1965	1844–1965		**Parish Magazines, 1966–78**
St James the Less, St James Avenue, Bethnal Green	1843–1956	1843–1950	1846–55	Banns, 1934–71, **Parish Magazines, 1903–80**
St James, Butcher Row, Ratcliffe	1840–1940	1840–1940		
St James, Curtain Road, Shoreditch	1839–1936	1841–1936		Banns, 1841–88
St John's, Bethnal Green	1837–1931	1837–1958	1847–55	Banns, 1837–1965, **Parish Magazines, 1973–83**
St John's, Cubitt Town, East Ferry Road	1872–1964	1875–1932		Confirmations, 1942–51
St John's, Limehouse Fields	1853–1955	1853–1940	1949–54	Banns, 1948–55, Confirmations, 1941–54
St John's, Wapping	1618–1940	1620–1940	1620–1958	
St John the Evangelist, Golding Street, Stepney	1870–1943	1870–1948		Banns, 1910–21
St John the Baptist, New North Road, Hoxton	1830–1932	1830–1947	1826–64	
St Jude's, Old Bethnal Green, Bethnal Green	1846–1945	1846–1951		**Parish Magazines, 1892–1919**
St Jude's, Commercial Street, Whitechapel	1848–1922	1848–1922		

St Katherine's by the Tower, Poplar	1914–46			
St Leonard's, Shoreditch	1558–1901	1698–1899	1558–1858	*Parish Magazines, 1931–88*
St Luke's Burdett Road, Limehouse	1869–1923	1872–1958		
St Luke's, West Ferry Road, Millwall, Isle of Dogs	1864–1964	1891–1952		Banns, 1961–4
St Mark's, St Mark's Gate, Shoreditch	1848–1917	1848–1933		
St Mark's, Goodman's Fields	1840–1926	1841–1926		
St Mark's, Victoria Park, Old Ford Road	1869–1952	1888–1955		Banns, 1896–1966
St Mary's, Bow Road, Stratford le Bow	1538–1956	1539–1968	1538–1862	Confirmations, 1883–91, **Parish Magazines, 1953–6**
St Mary's, Bromley High Street, Bromley St Leonard	1622–1960	1622–1960	1622–1866	**Parish Magazines, 1906–21**
St Mary's, Spitalfields Square, Stepney	1734–1911	1720–1911		Banns, 1875–1911, **Parish Magazines, 1883–1911**
St Mary's, Cable Street, Stepney	1850–1958	1850–1959		
St Mary's, High Street, Whitechapel	1558–1940	1558–1940	1558–1857	Banns, 1807–56

St Mary's, St Matthews Row, Bethnal Green	1746–1993	1746–1987	1746–1877	**Parish Magazines, 1971–93**, Confirmations, 1905–86, Banns, 1959–81
St Matthew's, Pell Street, Stepney	1859–91	1860–91		
St Matthew's, Salmon Lane, Limehouse Fields	1871–1947	1872–1954		Confirmations, 1895–1943, Parish Magazines, 1901–81
St Mary's, Britannia Walk, Hoxton	1866–1941	1873–1940		Banns, 1909–21
St Matthias, Cheshire Street, Bethnal Green	1842–1948	1848–1948		Banns, 1913–58
St Matthias, Woodstock Terrace, Poplar	1867–1976	1867–1976		Banns, 1900–76, **Parish Magazines, 1870, 1900–76**
St Michael's, Mark Street, Shoreditch	1863–1963	1865–1960		*Parish Magazines, 1943–7*
St Michael's and All Angels, St Leonard's Road, Bromley	1862–1948	1865–1973		
St Nicholas and All Hallows, Aberfeldy Street, Poplar	1900–41	1967		
St Olave's, Mile End New Town	1875–1914	1876–1914		
St Paul's, Dock Street	1848–1982	1864–1970		Banns, 1905–70, Confirmations, 1919–66

Religions in the East End

St Paul's, Virginia Road, Bethnal Green	1871–1948	1868–1947		
St Paul's, Bow Common	1858–1926	1859–1936		
St Paul's, Old Ford Street, St Stephens' Road	1878–1951	1879–1960		Banns, 1912–66
St Paul's, The Highway, Shadwell	1671–1927	1671–1934	1671–1903	Banns, 1822
St Peter's, Hoxton Square	1870–1919	1875–1937		Banns, 1875–1906
St Peter's, Garford Street, Limehouse	1866–1968	1888–1967		
St Peter's, London Docks, Shadwell	1857–1933	1867–1945		
St Peter's, St Peter's Avenue, Bethnal Green	1843–1911	1843–1914	1843–1955	**Parish Magazines, 1975–82**
St Peter's, Mile End Old Town	1839–1954	1840–1957		
St Phillip's, Swanfield Road, Bethnal Green	1842–1946	1843–1952		Confirmations, 1932–6
St Phillip's, Newark Street, Spitalfields	1838–1929	1845–1978		
St Saviour's, Hyde Road, Hoxton	1863–1943	1866–1948		Banns, 1893–1917
St Saviour's, Northumbria Street, Poplar	1874–1975	1875–1975		Banns, 1955–77, Confirmations, 1903–64, **Parish Magazines, 1901–31**

St Saviour and the Cross, Wellclose Square, Stepney	1857–68			
St Simon Zelote's, North Street, Bethnal Green	1847–1951	1847–1951		
St Stephen's, East India Docks, Poplar	1867–1940	1867–1947		Confirmations, 1918–49, **Parish Magazines, 1918–41**
St Stephen's, Tredegar Road, North Bow	1858–1961	1858–1961		Banns, 1956–82, **Parish Magazines, 1897–1930**
St Stephen's, Commercial Street, Spitalfields	1861–1930	1862–1929		Banns, 1920–1930
St Thomas, Baroness Road, Bethnal Green	1848–1919	1850–1911		
St Thomas, Arbour Square, Stepney	1840–1940	1840–1940		Banns, 1891–1940

Note: All the above archives are held at the LMA, those in **bold** are at THLHL&A; those in *italics* are at HA.

Wills are a key source for family history. Looking for those post-1858 is straightforward; indexes can be seen on Ancestry.co.uk, and copies can then be ordered online at www.wills.gov.uk. However, before 1858 the Church courts dealt with wills. It is well known that a principal court for wills being proved for property in the south of England was the Prerogative Court of Canterbury, 1383–1858. These can be searched on TNA's website Discovery and copies can be downloaded for a fee. Or they can be seen free of charge at a computer at TNA.

There were other courts, too. Relevant to this book's topic were the Commissary Court of London, 1374–1857. This dealt with property and goods in a number of parishes, including Bethnal Green, Bow, Bromley-

St John's church, Limehouse (collection of Paul Lang).

by-Bow, Limehouse, Poplar, St George-in-the-East, St Paul's Shadwell, Christ Church, Spitalfields, Stepney, Wapping and Whitechapel, with wills surviving from 1523 to 1857 with gaps. The Archdeaconry Court of London, 1393–1807 covered numerous London parishes including St Leonard's, Shoreditch, with wills surviving for 1524–1807. Although poor people, and especially women, are less likely to leave wills because they have nothing to bequeath (at this period a married woman's property belonged to her husband), these indexes are still worth checking, for sometimes even pauper inmates of workhouses were known to leave wills.

London wills, 1507–1858, can be searched on Ancestry.co.uk and the text seen. An example of an East Ender's will is as follows:

> In the Name of God, Amen.
>
> I, Anne Askew of Great Hermitage Street, Wapping, London, widow, being of sound mind and memory, but weak in body, do hereby make this my last Will and Testament, Imprimis, I recommend my soul unto Almighty God from whom I received it and my Body unto the Earth.
>
> I give and bequeath, after my just debts and funeral expenses are paid, unto Mrs Anna Lyall of Hewitts Court, Strand, all my wearing apparel & linen, and unto my Brother, Mr Lauchlan Monson of Shadwell shoemaker, all my household furniture and other affects I may be possessed of and whom I doe hereby appoint and constitute sole Execution of this my last Will and Testament.
>
> In witness whereof I have hereunto set my hand and seal in the presence of the undermentioned witnesses this 20 first day of July one thousand eight hundred and seven.
>
> Signed sealed and delivered in the presence of
> Henry Clark
> Mary Francis.

By the beginning of the twentieth century, although religion was still important, most East Enders did not attend church regularly. Walter Besant wrote,

> This does not indicate the hatred of religion ... it is simply indifference ... And although he does not go to church the East Londoner is by no means loath to avail himself of everything that can be got out of the church; he will cheerfully attend at concerts and limelight shows, his wife will cheerfully get what she can at a rummage sale.

Likewise children often did go, with attendance at Sunday School, Boys' and Girls' Brigades, Boy Scouts and Girl Guides, all groups linked with the churches, meaning that it was necessary to go to church. Churchgoing also brought other benefits, such as trips out and teas, so there was every incentive to join in. It also meant that their parents could have some time to themselves on Sundays.

There is only limited information about Sunday Schools. What there is includes, at THLHL&A, the annual returns for the East London Auxiliary Sunday School Union for 1892–8 and 1936–7, together with statistics on numbers in 1959. There are papers for St Stephen's church, north Bow, for 1907–8.

For the late nineteenth and twentieth centuries, parish magazines, produced on a monthly basis, can be a useful source of genealogical information. This is for two main reasons. First, these magazines included lists of all those people who held offices at the church, most of whom were lay people who held them as volunteers. These included Sunday school teachers, leaders of youth clubs, captains of the bells, leaders of uniformed associations affiliated with the Church, leaders of sports clubs and charities, secretaries of missionary societies as well as churchwardens and clergy. Perhaps your ancestor may have been one of these helpers. Since these are updated on a monthly basis, they will give fairly precise details as to when your ancestor began and finished in such a role. Secondly, the magazines give an impression of what the parish in all its guises did, and the monthly vicar's letter should note local concerns which had a spiritual dimension. If your ancestor was an East End clergyman, then these are of great interest. Some parish magazines are at THLHL&A, or with the main parish archives at the LMA (as noted in the table above); if the church still exists, though many do not, magazines may be held there, too.

The parish magazines for All Hallows Church, Bromley, list benefactors to the numerous local charitable causes: the rector's discretionary fund, the sick and poor fund, Christmas cheer and treats, sale of work, magazine fund, sale of work, goods for sale and several others. This is a useful way of finding whether your local ancestors, if relatively well off, were charitable (or not). Church members who were active in church work will be mentioned, as are baptisms, marriages and funerals.

Church archives are very variable; some may not be directly relevant because they will deal solely with the church fabric, its repairs and additions, unless your ancestor was involved in this. Others deal with people. These may be the archives of the church's decision-making bodies such as the Vestry and from the early twentieth century, the Parochial Church Council. Those parishioners attending these meetings will be listed and the decisions taken will be noted.

Archives of church youth and women's groups may also be important, for the same reason. For instance, at the LMA there is a Youth Fellowship logbook for St Dunstan's, Stepney, 1937–8 and Arbour Youth Club Centre for 1950–1 (P93/DUN/372).

Until the early nineteenth century the Anglican Church was a key part of the civil state as well as fulfilling its ecclesiastical role. Parishes played an important role in the poor law, the maintenance of law and order and the upkeep of roads and bridges within the parish (supervised at county level by the quarter sessions; in the case of the East End this was for the county of Middlesex).

Finally the role of the church courts, other than in the administration of wills, should be stated. Church courts had power over the laity from their inception in the Middle Ages until 1860 and still exist to deal with clerical offences. These courts punished what were deemed moral and religious offences, rather than criminal ones. So they would try people accused of adultery, witchcraft, heresy, blasphemy, incest, refusal to pay tithes and non-attendance at church. Those found guilty were given public shaming or at the most extreme, excommunication. The relevant court was the London Consistory Court, at its most powerful in the sixteenth and seventeenth centuries, and their archives are held at the LMA, which is the diocesan record office, as are most county record offices. The Act Books contain statements made both for and against the defendants' personal lives, thus providing a great deal of information about them. However, until 1733, most are written in Latin.

Act Books date from 1496 to 1765, mostly indexed from 1575. There are also Assignation Books, 1633–1855 (DL/AM), Sentences Books, 1670–1817 (DL/C-05), mostly in alphabetical order after 1670, Depositions, 1553–1806 (DL), indexed 1752–1806, Matrimonial Causes, 1821–1904 (DL/C-01), indexed by name, Answer Books (DL/C-06), 1617–1808.

The majority of parish archives are held at the LMA. This is because the county councils established record offices which began collecting archives before the borough libraries had established professional archives services. However, parts of some parish archives, particularly for the civil parish which dealt with the old poor law (as noted in chapter 3), are held at HA and THLHL&A. Churches have become far fewer in the twentieth century. Of the dozen which existed in Bethnal Green in 1850, only four remain as churches; two have been converted to use as housing and of the other six there is now no physical trace.

Nonconformity

Apart from the Church of England, there were numerous other denominations of Protestantism; principally Methodism, Baptism and Congregationalists. Unlike the Anglican Church they were independent of the civil state and therefore not involved in secular matters such as the poor law. From 1689 they were able to worship legally. They did conduct baptism and marriage services, but all burials had to be conducted in an Anglican church. Some Nonconformist registers for 1694–1921 can be searched for on Ancestry.co.uk. Many Nonconformist registers are held at TNA.

Unlike the case with Anglican archives, many are held locally. These churches also produced church magazines, but unlike the established church, they also they created membership registers. These listed the members of the church, with name, address and date of admission. They often noted if or when the member left the church, giving date and reason for departure.

At HA there are the following:

1. Harbour Light Methodist Church, Goldsmith's Row, Haggerston, Shoreditch, trustees' minutes, 1896–1961 (D/E/234C/1)
2. Hoxton Academy Chapel, Shoreditch, Sunday School records, 1815–1935 (D/E/248HOX)
3. Hoxton Market Christian Mission, Shoreditch, annual reports, mission magazines, photographs and programmes, 1900–83 (D/E248HCM, 2013/09)
4. Pownall Road Congregational church, Shoreditch, minutes and membership records, 1866–1950 (D/E/233/POW)

At THLHL&A are the following:

1. Little Alie Street Baptist Church, Wapping, membership registers, 1750–1899 (W/LA/S)
2. Poplar and Berger Baptist Tabernacle, quarterly magazines, 1961–5 (LC7033)
3. Stepney Meeting House, magazines, 1885–7 (L8779)
4. Stepney Meeting House and John Knox Presbyterian church, membership registers, 1644–1894 (W/SMH/A/6/1) and register of cancellations of church membership, 1894–1904 (W/SMH/A/6/10–11)
5. Trinity United Reformed (formerly Congregationalist) Church, Poplar, membership register, 1951–75 (W/TUC/1/5/1); magazines, 1872, 1936–7, 1952–3 (L502)
6. Victoria Park Baptist church, Bethnal Green, membership registers, c.1867–1986 (W/TUC/5/1/12–13)

As with the Anglican churches, a few Sunday School records exist; for Poplar Methodist church, 1891–1982 (W/PMC/7/3), for the Sunday School Union for the Good Shepherd Mission, Bethnal Green, Minute books for 1890–1931 (W/BGH/1/5/2) and for the Trinity United Reform church, 1922–39. Other archives are shown in the table.

Nonconformist church records

Church	Baptisms	Marriages	Burials
Bow Road Methodist Church, Poplar		1866–1916	1862–1955
Bromley Methodist church Dee Street	**1880–4**		
Bruce Road Congregational Church, Poplar		1935–41	
Brunswick Methodist Chapel, Limehouse	1909–54	1900–54	1831–53
Burdett Road, Congregational Church, Stepney		1909–39	
Cannon Street Congregational Church, Stepney	1792–1810		

Chrisp Street Primitive Methodist chapel, Bromley		1907–25	
Cubitt Town Methodist Church	1877–1935		
East London (Baptist) Tabernacle, Burdett Street		1923–41	
Edinburgh Castle, Methodist church, Mile End		1936–51	
Emery Hall Augusta Street, Poplar		1918–54	
Haggerston Methodist Mission, Shoreditch		*1938–86*	
Harley Street Congregational chapel, Bow	1876–1926	1876–1925	
John Knox Presbyterian Chapel, Stepney		1900–39, **1958–73**	
Latter Rain Outpouring Revival Church, Hoxton, Shoreditch		*1979–94*	
Lycett Memorial Baptist Church, Stepney	**1948–62**	1955–62	
Millwall United Reform church	1876–1937		
New Road Congregational Meeting House, Stepney	1785–1817		
Old Ford Methodist Chapel, Poplar			
Poplar Methodist Chapel	**1837–66**	1946–73	
Poplar Presbyterian Church, Plimsoll Street		1901–13	
St Columba's Presbyterian Church	1892–1962	1892–1939	
St George's Methodist Centenary Chapel	**1911–93**	**1955–87**	
Spitalfields Methodist Chapel	1838–46		
Stepney Meeting House		1918–74	1790–1853 (and index)

Welsh Methodist Church, Chiltern Road	1861–1933		
Victoria Park Congregational Church, Bethnal Green	1905–50		
Working Lads' Institute, Whitechapel Road, Stepney		1905–6	
White's Row Chapel, Spitalfields	1756–1908		
Wycliffe Congregational Church, Philpott Street, Stepney	1850–1906	1850–73	1831–1902

Registers are available on microfilm at the LMA, those in **bold** at THLHL&A and those in *italics* at HA.

Much of what has been said about Anglican churches as to the non-ecclesiastical dimension of these churches can be repeated here.

Catholicism

There were a number of Catholic churches in the East End. Parish magazines for the following exist at THLHL&A; Holy Name, Bow Common, 1985–7, Our Lady of the Assumption Church, 1967, St Mary and St Michael's, 1966–71. If your East End ancestors were Irish, then the archives of the Catholic churches are especially important, especially for baptisms and marriages. Many Catholic archives are held at the Westminster Diocesan Archives, 16A Abingdon Road, Kensington, London W8 6AF (tel. 020 7938 3580); email archivist@rcdow.org.uk.

The registers for Catholic churches are similar to those for the Protestant churches, but there are important differences, too. For baptism registers, date of birth is included, as is the maiden name of the mother and the names of the godparents, which is far more informative than those of other forms of Christianity. Burial registers include date of death as well as that of the burial service and sometimes even the location of the grave, if known.

For the purposes of this book, the relevant archives held at Westminster Diocesan Archives are as shown in table.

Records of Catholic churches

Church	Baptisms	Marriages	Burials/Confirmations
Commercial Road, SS Mary and Michael	1789–1800, 1832–40 (transcripts)	1832–9	1856–99
Mile End, Guardian Angels	1869–90	1904–62	
Poplar, SS Mary and Joseph's	1818–56 (transcripts)	1818–56 (transcripts)	
Underwood Road, St Anne's, Spitalfields	1848–1920 (indexed to 1909)	1851–90 (indexed to 1934)	1856–1931
Wapping St Patrick's	1871–1905		

There were also Catholic charity schools at Poplar, Blackwall and Limehouse, Whitechapel and Spitalfields. Their records are not held at the Westminster Diocesan Archives but, where they survive, at the schools and parishes themselves.

Other Christian Denominations

The Huguenots were French Protestants who were a major group in east London in the sixteenth to the eighteenth centuries and will be detailed in the next chapter. They worshipped in their own churches, several of which were located in the East End. The church registers have been transcribed and so are accessible in a number of the publications of the Huguenot Society. They include those for the French Church of Saint Jean, Spitalfields (1687–1827) in volume XXXIX, La Patente, Spitalfields (1689–1785) in volume XI and Hoxton, 1751–83, in volume XLV and the Church of the Artillery, Spitalfields, 1691–1786, in volume XLII. These register entries are in French, but the volumes are indexed. The Spitalfields project was an excavation of Christchurch, Spitalfields, between 1984–6 and this was where many Huguenots had been buried. The findings are explored in these two books: Margaret Cox's *Life and Death in Spitalfields, 1700–1850* (1996) and Jez Reeve and Max Adams' *The Archaeology across the Styx* (1993). Many Huguenots later attended Anglican churches when their own began to close due to falling congregations as the nineteenth century progressed, so you should check the registers for these, too.

The Germans of the East End had their own churches. The German Evangelical Reformed St Paul's church was founded in 1697 but moved to Hooper Square, Leman Street, Whitechapel, in 1819 and to Goulston Street in 1886–7. Registers of baptisms, marriages and burials are to be found at THLHL&A. Registers of St George's German Lutheran church, Alie Street (baptisms, 1763–1895, marriages, 1825–96, and burials, 1818–53) are available from the Anglo-German Family History Society. Those for St Boniface's Catholic church are also there (baptisms, 1809–1950, and marriages, 1864–1968), the originals still being held at the church. There are also extensive collections of other parish records for St Paul's and St George's churches at THLHL&A, too.

Non-Christian Religions

Judaism

There were several synagogues in the East End in the nineteenth and twentieth centuries. These include the Princelet Street Synagogue off Brick Lane, whose marriage (1877–1944) and burial records are located at THLHL&A, as are subscription books and marriage records for the Great Spitalfields Synagogue, 1909–47, and membership lists for the Philpot Street Sephardic Synagogue for 1938–9. Marriage authorisation indexes for 1845–1908 can be found on the United Synagogue website (www.theus.org.uk) and this includes the East London Synagogue at Stepney. Copies of certificates for these marriages can then be purchased. Marriage Notice Books for Stepney from 1926 onwards and for Bethnal Green for 1837–78 and 1920–65 can be viewed at THLHL&A. These books give names, address and age of the parties intended for marriage, the length of time that they have lived in Britain and the proposed place of marriage.

The archives of the Spanish and Portuguese Jewish Synagogue, Bevis Marks, has been deposited at the LMA, but access is via the written permission of the depositor only. These archives include: births, 1767–1882 (indexed), circumcisions, 1715–85, 1803–25, 1855–9; marriage contracts, 1690–1795, and burials, 1657–1735 (indexed). Some of these have been transcribed and are available at THLHL&A. Records for the Great Synagogue, Dukes's Place, Aldgate, for 1795–1872 can be seen on microfilm there.

A list of synagogues is available at http://www.jewishgen.org/jcr-uk/london/east-end-addresses.htm.

Bevis Marks synagogue (photo by the author).

Islam

There are a number of mosques in the East End, mostly established in very recent decades. For example, the East London Mosque on Whitechapel Road was built in 1982–5 and the London Jamme Masjid

Jamme Masjid Mosque, Shoreditch (photo by Paul Lang).

(Great Mosque) on Fournier Street/Brick Lane dates from 1975 and is in a former Huguenot church. None of their archives have yet been deposited in a public place, presumably because of their relative recent date range and because of a reluctance to deposit on the part of the institutions themselves, lacking a tradition of doing so. However, many archives of the East London Mosque are being made available to bona fide researchers and arrangements are being made to house these safely. See http://www.eastlondonmosque.org.uk/content/east-london-mosque-london-muslim-centre-archive-collections.

Chapter 7

MOVING IN – AND OUT – OF THE EAST END

The East End of London has long been a destination for migrants, perhaps more so than elsewhere in London. In part this was because of its geographical situation, being physically nearer Europe and elsewhere than other parts of London, in part due to there being sources of employment there and opportunities for the enterprising, and also because it was just outside the City boundaries and so was free from guild restrictions prevalent there. The Huguenots from France in the sixteenth and seventeenth centuries, the Jews from Eastern Europe and Russia in the nineteenth century and the Bangladeshis in the twentieth are perhaps the three main peoples who have made the East End their home, though there were others from abroad as well. Of course many people moved there from elsewhere in the British Isles, too, including from Ireland in the eighteenth and nineteenth centuries. But it is also a place that people have moved away from in large numbers, especially since 1945. This chapter is devoted to sources for secular archives as those for religious bodies have been covered in chapter 6. However, perhaps until the 1970s, the level of immigration should not be exaggerated, as Simon Webb recalled, 'I grew up and attended a number of schools in the East End [in the 1960s] and did not speak to a single black person until I had left school. This was not because I was a racist bigot; it is simply that there was not a single black or Asian person in any of my classes.'

There are a number of general sources that can be used for those arriving prior to the twentieth century. *Register of Aliens, 1523–1625*, published as volume 10 by the Huguenot Society in 1900, giving names of foreigners in the capital and the taxes paid by them ('alien' was a term for a foreigner). Then there were three surveys of aliens living in London, two in 1571 and one in 1618. These can be viewed at TNA in SP 12/82 and 84 and in SP 14/102.

Other sources include the indexes to the Calendars to State Papers Domestic (1509–1704) at TNA, and also the Calendars to Treasury Papers; again available at TNA and the British Library. Passes for incoming people in the eighteenth century were issued by the Secretaries of State, and noted in SP 44/386–411 for 1697–1784 and FO 366/544 for 1748–94. There are some indexes to these; in the aforementioned State Papers calendars, up to 1704, then in the Calendar of Home Office Papers, 1760–75. The political turmoil caused by the French Revolution in 1789 led to a new surge of refugees from France, this time escaping political, not religious terror. Some returns to the Aliens' Office for 1810–11 survive at FO 83/21–2. Newcomers from 1793 to 1836 were subject to the 1793 Aliens Act, but very few records survive. Newcomers had to register with the Justices of the Peace, giving name, address, rank and occupation. This information was sent in the form of certificates to the Home Office. After 1826, such records are found in HO 2, and are indexed up to 1849 in HO 5/25–32. There is an index at TNA for the names of Poles and Germans who arrived from 1847 to 1852. No certificates survive after 1852.

Class HO 3 contains lists of alien passengers made by masters of ships arriving at English ports, for 1836–69, with a gap for 1861–6. They are arranged chronologically and there were four lists per year. They give name, profession and country of origin, name of ship travelled in and port of arrival. Alien arrivals for 1810–11 and 1826–69 can be searched online by name at Ancestry.co.uk.

There were relief efforts directed to Spanish and Polish refugees in the later nineteenth century. For the Spanish, TNA, PMG 53/1–9 cover payments from 1855 to 1909 when the last one died. For the Polish, PMG 53/2–8 cover allowances given from 1860 to 1899 and T 50/81–97 for the years 1841–56.

Naturalisation

Many immigrants became legally British subjects by either receiving letters of denization or, in later centuries, by being naturalised. This meant that they had all the privileges of natural born Britons, which included voting rights. Letters of denizen exist from the sixteenth century, when about 7,000 were granted. These are in the publications of the Huguenot Society, volumes 8, 18 and 27, *Letters of Denization and Acts of Naturalisation for Aliens in England*, covering 1509–1603, 1603–1700 and 1701–1800 respectively. The latter two volumes also cover Ireland.

Another good, general source is the shipping registers of incoming passengers from 1890 to 1960. These cover ships travelling from outside Europe only. They can be searched on Ancestry.co.uk and give the name, age and profession of the immigrant/traveller and their expected address if known. You will also learn when the ship left, its name and port of arrival, together with the class that they travelled on. There are no equivalent sources for air passengers.

Huguenots

Most of those arriving in Britain before the nineteenth century were from the European Continent. These were French Huguenots and German Protestants who were fleeing religious tyranny in their home Catholic states, though some were what would now be called 'economic refugees'. Some locals welcomed new arrivals, especially if they looked as if they would be of benefit to the state. French Huguenots, suffering from religious persecution in France in the late sixteenth and late seventeenth century, were welcomed partly on religious and ideological grounds, but also because many of them were skilled workers in the silk industry and could make financial contributions to the Exchequer. Many settled in Bethnal Green and Spitalfields. Some joined the British Army and it is estimated that, in the eighteenth century, 10 per cent of colonels were of Huguenot stock, including Jean Ligonier (1680–1770), commander in chief in the Seven Years War.

They are well known in part because of the work of the Huguenot Society, in publishing and indexing relevant records. Many of these are church registers as noted in chapter 6. Secular records include volume XVIII, *Letters of Naturalisation for Aliens, 1603–1700*, XXXIII, *Extracts from the Court Books of the Weavers' Company of London*, XLIX, *Relief of French Protestants, 1681–87*. There is also volume LII, covering the archives of the French Protestant Hospital, La Providence (1798–1957) and the Coqueau charity (1745–1901), including details of applicants.

Huguenots in London tended to settle in Spitalfields and Soho. The Huguenot Society (www.huguenotsociety.org.uk) can be contacted directly about Huguenot ancestors (for a fee), or you can see the published documents at TNA or Guildhall Libraries. Those with Huguenot ancestors should view http://huguenot.netnation.com to exchange information with those who can trace their line back to France.

Other sources, located at THLHL&A, include a register of a local friendly society which provided financial assistance for members in times of need. There is also an index to the Bethnal Green Protestant Dissenters' Burial Ground, Gibraltar Road, in use from 1792 to 1855 (TNA has the original) and many Huguenots were buried here. There was the Maison de Charitie at Spitalfields to assist destitute Huguenots and surviving records from 1739–41 were published in the Huguenot Society record series, volume LV. Records of the Huguenot Friendly Benefit Society from 1797–1912 are at the LMA (CLC/144). By the nineteenth century most of the descendants of the Huguenots had integrated into mainstream British society and there is now no identifiable Huguenot community in England.

Home of Mendosa the Jew, Bethnal Green (photo by the author).

Jewish Sources

Jews have lived in the East End since the late seventeenth century, once they were legally admitted back into England in 1657, though they remained in relatively small numbers. In the later nineteenth century there was a series of pogroms against the Jews living in the Russian Empire. Many of these people who were persecuted fled to more liberal countries such as Britain and the USA.

Apart from all the sources outlined above there are some which specifically relate to Britain's Jews. So great was the influx of often poverty-stricken Jews into Whitechapel, Spitalfields and Bethnal Green from the 1870s onwards that the Poor Jews' Temporary Shelter was established at Leman Street in Whitechapel. Each ship carrying Jews which arrived in London was met and adult men were greeted by a representative of the shelter. The records of those men who accepted shelter and help between 1895 and 1914 have been entered into a database (http://chrysalis.itsuct. ac.za/shelter/shelter.htm) and as there are over 43,000 names therein, it is well worth a look. A similar institution was the soup kitchen for the Jewish poor, founded in Spitalfields in 1854, and whose archives are located at the LMA.

There were two main London schools which catered for Jewish children. The most important was the Jews' Free School. The admission and discharge registers for the school, showing details of pupils and other archives from 1791 to 1999 (LMA/4046 and 4290) are held at the LMA. The Westminster Jews' Free School (LMA 4047) has deposited its records (1846–1950) at the LMA.

Those with Jewish roots should check www.jgsgb.org.uk and www. jewishgen.org. Most seventeenth-century Jewish immigrants were wealthy merchants from southern European countries. In the following century they mostly came from central and eastern Europe.

The *Jewish Chronicle* is a weekly newspaper founded in 1841 and is for Jews throughout Britain. Given the concentration of Jews in the East End it is a natural source of information and family notices. Copies are held on microfilm at THLHL&A. The newspaper has a national coverage and news about Jews overseas, but there is information about the East End, such as reports about the Poor Jews' Temporary Shelter. Allied to these are two useful books, *Jewish Victorian Genealogical Information from Jewish Newspapers, 1861–1870* and *1871–1880*, compiled by Doreen Bergen in 1999. These provide alphabetical lists of Jews mentioned in the press and the source reference.

Another source is the Annual Returns of the St George's Jewish Settlement, covering 1919–34, to be found on the shelves of the THLHL&A's library. This was a charitable organisation for young Jews, focusing on education and recreation. Although it does not mention individual youths, it does show the range of activities that adolescents could participate in. As befitted a charity, it also listed those who gave money to pay for its work, on an annual basis, and so lists of Jewish and other benefactors appear, together with the sums they gave. Annual reports of other Jewish organisations can also be seen at THLHL&A.

Journals of the Jewish Historical Society of England from 1896 to date and the *Jewish Year Book* from the same year are also worth a look. Both are annual and national publications. The former contains essays on numerous subjects relevant to British Jewish history. The latter lists synagogues, societies, clubs, schools, charities and unions. There are numerous books about the Jews in the East End and these are listed in the bibliography.

Many Jews left Whitechapel and Spitalfields in the mid-twentieth century. They had become more prosperous than their forebears and preferred to live in more attractive parts

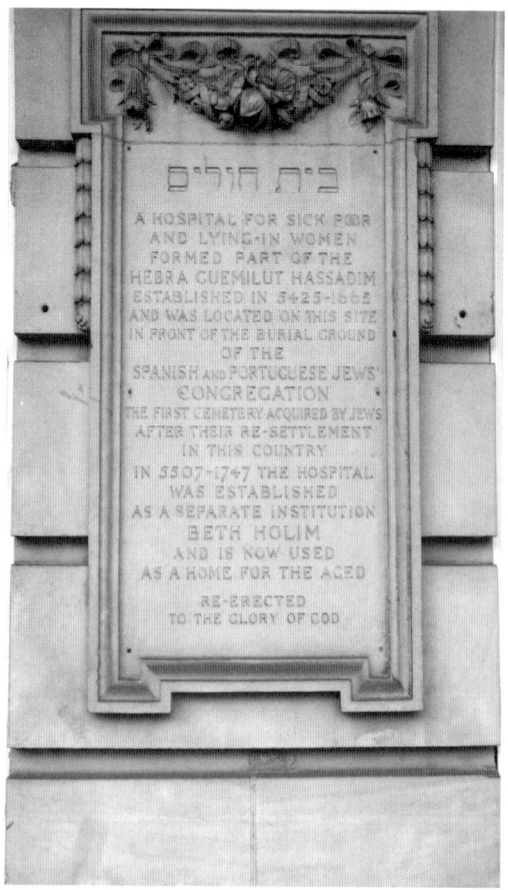

Memorial; to Jewish Hospital and Cemetery (photo by the author).

of London, especially north London or in Essex. Today there are very few Jews in the East End, yet their history there is very well documented and written about compared to any other immigrant group.

Irish

It was commonplace for the Irish to be working in the East End three centuries ago, as noted by Sir Robert Walpole in 1736: 'greater numbers than ordinary, as is said, of Irish being here, and not only working at hay and corn harvest, as has been usual, but letting themselves out to all sorts of labour considerably cheaper than the English labourers have and numbers of them being employed by the weavers upon the like terms'. Bow and Bromley were particularly popular places for Irish arrivals in the nineteenth century. Many were involved in working in the docks or in the construction and building trade (by undercutting workmen building St Leonard's church in Shoreditch in 1736 they provoked a riot and the military had to be called to restore order). There are no specific Irish sources for the East End. Catholic church and school archives are the main source for researchers; see chapter 6. Many Irish lived in Ratcliff, Wapping and Shadwell.

Germans

Although there have been Germans resident in London since the Middle Ages, as with the Jews, their numbers soared in the later nineteenth century. In 1851 there were 9,566 and in 1891 this number had nearly trebled. Some were German Jews. Some migrants were looking for work in business and industry, whilst others fled political persecution or to avoid conscription into the army. Although they represented numerous professions, they were concentrated in the East End sugar refining industry, which was centred in Stepney, known as Little Germany. As with other immigrant communities they had their own places of religion; for information about these see chapter 6 and for useful reference material see the bibliography. Many Germans were interned during the First World War and the relatively few archives referring to individuals which survive are held at TNA. There are also registers listing relief to these people among the Bethnal Green Union archives at the LMA. The Anglo-German Family History Society (www.agfhs.org./site/index.

php) should also be worth contacting. As with the Huguenots and Jews there is now very little trace of the Germans in the East End.

Chinese

Limehouse was the centre of London's China Town in the late nineteenth and twentieth centuries. Although they have left a trace in the popular fiction of thrillers by Sax Rohmer and others (from Agatha Christie to Dr Who), there is little specifically about them. References can be found in the local press (in 1941 a Chinese sailor was arrested for breaking food regulations) and the general sources such as the census and, for businesses, directories. Walter Besant discusses the Chinese in the East End in the late nineteenth century and found their number to be small; the opium den he visited was far from the den of vice as portrayed by the popular press.

The LMA holds two DVDs concerning the Chinese in London from 1900 to 1950 at LMA/4534/01/01/001, which were created in 2005. As with the Jews, there is now no trace of the Chinese in the East End, for the centre of Chinese life in London shifted in the post-war years westwards to Westminster, and China Town, now bigger than ever, is now located in Soho. The news cuttings files at THLHL&A are very extensive for the Chinese in the East End.

The Indian Subcontinent and Somalia

Mass migration is a post-war phenomenon, though there were Asian sailors in the East End prior to 1945 (some being noted as early as the seventeenth century). Then there were people from India in the 1950s onwards. From the 1970s, people from Bangladesh began to form a community in Spitalfields, especially around Brick Lane. This was known as Banglatown. Although they now make up about a third of the population of Tower Hamlets and form a larger percentage of the total than the Jews ever did, there is little in the way of records for the history of individuals, save for general sources such as Indian Year Books, the weekly newspaper *The Eastern Eye*, established in 1989, and electoral registers. However, there are a number of studies and oral histories which can be accessed at THLHL&A. These include: 'The Bengali East End' (oral history, 2011),

Brick Lane, 2017 (photo by the author).

'Don't just live, live to be remembered: The Somali East End' (2012–13). Two general websites worth exploring are www.swadhinata.org.uk, a London based Bengali heritage group which details organisations, events and individuals relevant to Bengali history in Britain. More generally there is www.open.ac.uk/researchprojects/makingbritain/ which deals with south Asians in Britain from 1870 to 1945. THLHL&A have little in the way of archival sources but do have a collection of pamphlets and news cuttings about this relatively new community in the East End. Newspapers and court records could be used to document community resistance to the National Front and other extremists in the 1970s. There are also a considerable number of Bengali newspapers held at THLHL&A.

Don't forget that all these immigrants should appear in many other records mentioned throughout this book: school and hospital registers, electoral registers, directories, military and tax records, newspapers and many more.

Although many people have moved in to the East End, many have moved out, too. The census statistics speak for themselves; in 1931 there

Bangladeshi shop, Mile End Road, 2017 (photo by the author).

were in the boroughs of Poplar, Stepney and Bethnal Green 488,521 people; in 1951 the total was 230,790. Some of these had been killed in the war, but only a relative minority. There had been a drift away from the East End before 1939, with people moving to neighbouring parts of east or north London or further afield, especially Essex. That trickle now became a flood. Although there was a study in 1957 about the changing patterns of family life in and away from the East End, as noted already, there seems to have been no extensive study of this huge social change. The materials for such a study would include inspection of electoral registers, rate books, census statistics (as census returns themselves are closed for a century) and oral history interviews. It is a study which awaits a researcher or even a team.

Chapter 8

LEISURE ACTIVITIES

Working hours were long and so it is not surprising that East Enders played as hard as they worked. In many ways our ancestors were a lot more sociable than we are, certainly on a face-to-face basis, seeking entertainment outside the home. Lacking televisions, home music systems or computers – or even proper lighting and heating enabling the home to be a source of rest, relaxation and entertainment, going out was far more common. Clubs and societies flourished, as did public meetings for religious, charitable and political purposes. One form of entertainment that the East End was known for was the music hall, especially from the early nineteenth century to the post-war years.

Local newspapers carried adverts for the music halls, listing the entertainers, times of performances and price of seats. These would vary over the weeks, of course. The *East London Observer* carried an advert for the People's Palace on Mile End Road for Saturday 29 January 1916. The performance began at seven that evening and entry cost 3 pence. Front seats were extra: 6 pence or a shilling. The entertainment included acts by Mr Arthur Bullivant, magician and ventriloquist, Mr Arthur Thomas, musical entertainer, Master Eric Brooks, 'the celebrated boy singer', Miss Alice Lilley, a soprano, and Miss Susette Tari and Mr Tom Copeland, both described as vocal and comedy entertainers.

At HA is a special collection of theatre bills (listing the performers and performances for particular nights), posters and cuttings. These include matter for the Britannia Theatre, Hoxton, the Grecian Theatre, Shoreditch, the National Standard Theatre and the Varieties Theatre, also in Shoreditch.

Street melody (collection of Lindsay Siviter).

There is a website devoted to music hall performers, at www.rhul.ac.uk/drama/music.hall/index.asp, which is a searchable list of entertainers from 1865 to 1890, stating role, date and place of entertainer. Other relevant websites are www.elta-project.org which covers the East London Theatre archive and the more general www.theatredatabase.com.

The LMA has a large collection of material about music halls and theatres because the LCC, and before 1889 the Middlesex justices, were the licensing authorities who decided whether to grant and renew licences for such places of entertainment (licensing archives for 1752–1888 are at MR/L/MD and for 1889–1960 at LCC/PC/ENT/02). The minute books include information about them, together with plans (GLC/AR/BR/19) and photographs, which can be searched for in the LMA's online catalogue.

At the dawn of the twentieth century, the cinemas began to challenge the music halls as the place to go for cheap, popular entertainment and for some decades they both coexisted. Directories list cinemas, or picture palaces as they were often termed, and by ascertaining those closest to where your ancestors lived you should be able to make an educated guess as to which they went to. Weekly cinema going was a popular pastime, especially among the young who wanted privacy for a short time. Initially quite small places, seating only a few hundred, by the 1920s and 1930s many expanded or new and larger cinemas were built.

To have a flavour of what your ancestors might have experienced, one good source of information is the local press. Adverts for the forthcoming week's films would appear there, perhaps with a review of the films, many of which may be wholly unknown now. An example is when the People's Palace cinema advertised in 1915. On Saturday 6 February, at eight o'clock, could be seen 'Animated Pictures' including *The Warwick Chronicle*. Doors opened at half past seven and seats cost either 3 or 6 pence. Films up to 1929 were silent but there was usually a pianist to provide musical accompaniment to the film and stars in the 1910s–1920s included Charlie Chaplin, Buster Keaton and Laurel and Hardy.

There were numerous public houses in the East End, not all of which now survive. Confusingly, many have been renamed throughout their history. The directories will enable you to identify those closest to where your ancestors lived and it may well have been the case that they patronised these. Pubs sometimes advertised in the local press, stating the name and address of the establishment, together with the name of the manager and the owner. Maps will show the location of pubs, but will rarely name them; you will need a contemporary directory to do that by cross-referencing it with the map.

Photographs of many of these establishments can be found on the THLHL&A website as well as at the THLHL&A, and also at HA. The LMA has a substantial photograph collection, too, and these can often be copied to help bring your ancestors' world to life.

The website www.pubshistory.com is worth viewing. It gives national coverage, but includes information on defunct pubs as well as current ones, showing changes of name and address as well as providing photographs. It is constantly being added to. Focusing solely on London is www.londonpublichouse.com.

Comments about pubs by contemporaries are also worth reading for the insights they provide. Charles Booth, a noted social observer at the end of the nineteenth century, had this to say:

> Anyone who frequents public houses will know that actual drunkenness is very much the exception ... Go into any of these houses – the ordinary public house at the corner of any ordinary East End street – there, standing at the counter, or seated on the benches against the wall or partition, will be perhaps, half a dozen people, men and women, chatting together over their beer – more often beer than spirits – or you may see a few men come in with no time to lose, briskly drink their glass and go. Behind the bar will be a decent middle aged woman, something above her customers in class, very decently dressed, respecting herself and respected by them. The whole scene is comfortable and quiet and orderly. To these houses those who live nearby send their children with a jug as readily as they would send them to any shop. (quoted in Jane Cox, *London's East End: Life and Traditions*, 1994, p. 182)

Old Blue Last pub, Shoreditch (photo taken by Paul Howard Lang, 2017).

There were clubs and societies catering to children and adults. Some of these have left archives behind them and so can be viewed. Minute books are very useful for showing the activities that occurred. Membership lists are of obvious use for family historians, for they can show names, addresses and even when the individual joined and when they left. Minute books are also useful if your ancestor was one of the committee which ran the club, if only to know where they were and what they were doing on particular evenings.

A number of records of clubs and societies are held at THLHL&A. These include those of the Brady Boys' Club, Whitechapel (S/BRA/1–2), including record cards, 1942–67 (closed until 2052), the New Cambridge Boys' Club, including membership records for 1930–64 (S/NCB/1-5), listing names, address, date of birth, schools attended, club classes attended (closed until 2025) and the records, 1947–75, of the Women's Own Club, part of the Lighthouse Baptist Church in Bromley by Bow (W/LBC/F/1).

Others at THLHL&A include magazines created by clubs and societies. These are the Bethnal Green Literary Society, 1907–11, Bethnal Green Men's Institute, 1934, 1938–9, and the East London Schools Athletics Association Sports, 1928–36. As with parish and works magazines they may mention your ancestor but if not will give an idea as to the activities he/she may have been involved in. For social historians they give evidence for what these clubs did and what they deemed important.

Local newspapers also covered the activities of such organisations. They tend to focus on special events, meetings and activities, especially those open to the public. These can include fundraising events and concerts, annual outings and so on. Sports clubs' matches are regularly reported and, apart from a write up of the match, usually list team members and the goals/runs etc. scored. The *East End News* in 1887 reported on the activities of the East London Protestant Defence League, the Poplar Conservative Association's annual excursion – to Buckhurst Hill with their 300 members – and that of the Poplar Liberal and Radical Association's trip to Chingford and their annual meeting (they had 700 members). The Poplar Constitutional Club and the Poplar Benevolent and Accidental Relief Society had their activities reported and the names of leading members were mentioned. Churches and workplaces also had a social dimension. These are often detailed in their official magazines and can feature in the press, too.

Parks

One source of leisure that was free to use were the parks. In the nineteenth century, with the growth of London, open spaces became fewer and fewer. Councils began to buy land for use for public recreation. Sports and games, organised or not, began to be played therein. However, few were established in the nineteenth-century East End compared to more prosperous parts of the capital (there were none in Shoreditch until after 1945) but more appeared after 1945 as land became available due to buildings being bombed and town planning schemes making them integral. Newspapers and Council Minutes provide good sources about activity in parks; whilst photographs provide the visual picture.

The East End's first park was the Victoria Park, established in 1842. The *Shoreditch Observer* of 28 October 1865 described it thus:

> The origin of Victoria Park was this. In the fourth and fifth year of her present Majesty's reign, an act was passed to enable the Commissioners of Woods and Forests to complete the sale of York House, and to purchase with the proceeds a royal park. The Duke of Sutherland paid £72,000 for the remainder of the lease of that house, and this money was applied to the purchase of that 200 acres of land situated in the parishes of St. John's, Hackney, St. Matthew's, Bethnal Green and St. Mary's Stratford le Bow, county of Middlesex. Nearly one thirds of the acreage mentioned is taken for building ground, the rest is Victoria Park. Its state previously had been market gardens and brickfields. The ornamental lake is made over the rough brickfield, near to which stood Bishop Bonner's famous hall. The park is bordered to the north side by Hackney; on the south by Sir G. Duckett's Canal, running nearly east and west; and on the west by the Regent's Canal. It is divided into two portions – the ornamental, or west part, and the east part. In the former there is an ornamental lake, being about 10 acres of surface, with 30 pretty islands. Here boats are hired out at 1s per hour, and there is a number of water fowl of various kinds. On the south west of the lake there is a fine avenue of elm trees, with a carriage drive and shady walks, there is also an arcade here, furnished with seats. On the north west side of the lake there is a handsome walk, called 'The Vale', which is planted with choice trees, shrubs and flowers. Close adjacent are the green houses and pits for raising and wintering the plants, but they look scarcely large enough for the purpose. In this portion of the park are several separate flower gardens, riband borders 300 yards long, and mixed flower beds of considerable extent, filled with various plants. The east park is used for games and contains two bathing lakes, which are well supplied with water. These are much frequented, as many as 7,000 people having bathed there in one morning. They are open, from four to eight o'clock pm. Every means is taken to ensure the safety of the bathers. Buoys are fixed, showing the depth

of water, there is a boat with a man ready to and if necessary, and the swimming master, Woodridge, is always in attendance. The extent of these two lakes is about six acres.

At the extreme end of the park is a cricket ground, of 38 or 40 acres. Here 60 or 80 wickets are often pitched on Saturdays. The ground is rolled and mown with a machine. About one third of the way through the park is the Victoria Drinking Fountain, presented by Miss Burdett Coutts; and to add to the means afforded for public exercise and recreation, there is a gymnasium, as there are also swings and merry-go-rounds.

There are references in the local press to the sports played there and the controversies that sometimes ensued because of them. Not all who visited them went there to be physically active, but merely to sit and stare, as with Emanuel Litvinoff and a friend, shortly before the Second World War:

> One Sunday morning that autumn, we trailed two laughing girls in Victoria Park. They sat on a bench by the lake, rubbed their mouths with lipsticks and looked at us in their tiny mirrors. One girl lifted her legs and crossed her knees. Morry dug his hands deeply into his pocket and caught his lower lip between his teeth. He stared sadly and vacantly at the muddy green water.
>
> 'Did you notice that movement?' he said in a hoarse voice. 'She's got good legs' I replied miserably. 'They swell up nice at the top'.
>
> We shivered and became silent. The girl twisted her slender ankle, glanced at her friend and spoke in an undertone. They both laughed.

The East End has a tradition of radical politics, and in the twentieth century political involvement was a popular pastime for many who were not professional politicians. George Lansbury, leader of the Labour Party in 1932–5 cut his teeth as a councillor for Bow and Poplar. As with the churches, party membership was as much a gateway to social activities for the whole family. Apart from the press, where these events were reported, there are numerous archives to document local party activity. At THLHL&A, there are many Labour Party archives from the 1930s–1990s. These include those for the North East Bethnal Green Labour Party, 1934–69 (S/LAB/B/1/1-4), the Limehouse Ward Labour Party, 1971–84 (S/LAB/E), the minute books for the branches of the Labour Party in Poplar from 1939–78 (S/LAB/D), and for the party in Shadwell ward from 1933–86 (S/LAB/G). There are some minutes and correspondence of the

The fountain, Victoria Park (collection of the author).

Tower Hamlets Labour Party from the 1960s to the 1980s (S/LAB/K). None of these include membership lists, annoying as this will be to family historians, but as with church minute books, they will list committee members and refer to their activity, as well as to events and resolutions passed. Disappointingly, perhaps, there is very little archival information for the Communist Party in the East End; this is limited to various papers from the 1930s and 1940s (LC7437–8), including plans for the future.

From the late nineteenth century there were organised youth activities. Very few of these refer to specific individuals, however. A rare example, at THLHL&A, is the Boys' Brigade Company Roll book for the 109th London Company for Bethnal Green, covering 1945–6 (W/GSM/4/6). This lists members, with name, rank, address and attendance at drill and Bible lessons noted. Archives of East End Scout groups include those of the Poplar Scouts, minute book, 1945–59 (S/MIS/5), papers of the 34th Stepney Scout Group for 1962–71, and at HA, papers of the 17th Shoreditch Scouts, focusing on camps and activities, 1952–7 (D/E/21/AUG/2) and the minute book for the 1st Shoreditch Scouts, 1962–72. There seems to be virtually nothing on the activities of the Girl Guides or the Girls' Brigades, though the archives of many uniformed youth organisations are housed in central archives at their headquarters.

Of course many children made their own entertainment independent of organisations. There is very little that can be known about these except what is revealed in memoirs of East End Life. The author of a 1960s East End childhood discusses playing on bomb sites (those who have seen the 1946 film *Hue and Cry* will remember scenes of children playing in bombed-out buildings in post-war East London) and on the railway lines. All completely unsupervised, of course.

Many East Enders took the opportunity to leave their neighbourhood when the possibility arose. Day trips to Hampstead Heath and Epping Forest, or further afield to Southend, were favoured pleasure spots and Besant discusses these in his East London book. Hop picking was another popular pastime which mixed work with leisure for many East End women in the summers of the nineteenth and early to mid-twentieth centuries. Women would go down to the hop fields in Kent to work on the farms there, often with children in tow, sleeping in barns, and their menfolk would join them at the weekends. There are a number of books and photographs about hop pickers at the THLHL&A. Besant wrote, 'The hopping, considered as an amusement ... especially if the weather is fine, it is amusement with profit; the hoppers come home with a pocketful of money ... with the highest spirits possible', though he adds that on occasion there was trouble with the law. In this case, the Kentish press would doubtless be a useful source of information.

Chapter 9

SCHOOLING AND HEALTH

Both schools and hospitals were initially founded by charitable benefactors, but by the nineteenth century the state at a local level began to make provision for those in need, paid for by the ratepayers. The two systems ran in tandem, but by the twentieth century the state began to assert more and more control over welfare.

Schools

Early schools were either privately run for profit or were charity schools. Shoreditch parish ran charity schools for almost two centuries, and the school minutes ran from 1705 to 1888 and are held at HA. Until 1880 schooling was not compulsory.

Records of charity schools can often be found at local record offices:

1. Hoxton Academy Chapel Sunday School, Shoreditch, minutes, cash books, girls' register, 1814–1901
2. Shoreditch Charity Schools, minutes, reports, subscribers and admissions lists, 1705–1898 (D/E/248/HOX).

At THLHL&A are:

1. Register of subscribers to the Ratcliff Charity School, 1851–9 (I/HRS/7/1)
2. Minute book of subscribers to the Poplar and Blackwall National School, 1804–31 (I/PBN)
3. Minute books of the Ratcliff Charity School, 1806–19 (I/MSS)
4. Mile End Old Town Charity School minutes, 1771–1809 (I/MEO)

5. Middlesex Charity Schools, St George in the East, 1806–1819 (I/MSS)

The state began to be involved in education from 1833. Initially this was in the way of providing grants to existing bodies to run schools. These were the National schools, run by the Church of England. These helped inculcate an Anglican version of Christianity. There were also the British schools which were Nonconformist.

In 1870 the Forster Education Act decreed that schooling become universal and that schools be built and run at public expense where there were insufficient existing in a district. Boards of Education were created to administer these schools where religion was taught non-denominationally. For London, this was the city-wide London School Board, from 1870 to 1903. By 1880 schooling was compulsory until the age of 10; this rose to 12 in 1902 and 14 in 1918.

From 1904 to 1965 the LCC was the educational authority for the schools in inner London and that includes the East End; it was replaced by the Inner London Educational Authority up to 1990 when London boroughs became responsible for the state schools within their boundaries. State school archives for the East End schools that have been deposited by the schools were therefore held at the LMA, not the local history centres, but this policy has changed now and so school records should be increasingly be deposited at local record offices.

The easiest way to search for information about your ancestor's schooldays is to go to Ancestry.co.uk and search London School Admissions and Discharges, 1840–1911. This is a database of school admission registers held at the LMA. This will provide the following information: name of pupil, date of birth, date of admission, name of school, father's name and address, and date of departure, as noted by the following example: Margaret Baldock, a pupil of Berner Street School, pupil number 901. Admitted on 17 January 1893, father was William, a railway guard of 4 Severne Street. Born 7 July 1886 and left the school on 10 April 1893.

Punishment books are another source which lists names of pupils. These are arranged chronologically and list pupil, date of punishment, number of strokes inflicted and the reason for the punishment. Corporal punishment was banned in schools in 1986, but the practice had fallen into infrequency by the 1970s and fewer names then appear. The records

St John's Wapping Charity School (photo by Paul Lang).

are closed for a century, but you should be able to view any punishments which occurred prior to 1918. Relatively few names, proportionately, appear and expect repeat offenders. However, if these still exist they are worth viewing.

Another type of school record with lengthy closure periods is the Honour Books, which list especially good deeds performed by pupils.

School magazines can also shed light on those attending school, though they focus on members of the school sports teams and the senior members of the school clubs. Exam successes and prizes awarded will be reported. There might be accounts of school trips and writings by pupils (stories and poetry) might also feature here. Most pupils will not be mentioned, and any hint of wrongdoing will be suppressed.

The Parmiter school (Bethnal Green) magazine for 1920 was a quarterly publication. It listed boys who had left the school, by class, those who had just enrolled, with surname and initials. There was information about former pupils who had died or otherwise served in the Great War. For Prize days, there is a list of pupils who were awarded prizes for achievement in various sports, shooting, swimming and gym. There are lists of the cricket and football teams. There are also reports of house activities, and letters from Old Boys either at university or in the armed forces.

The LCC awarded medals for good conduct, attendance and achievement. There are certificates for attendance for 1887–9 and 1915–18, and listings of rewards for attendance, 1905–11, at the LMA (LCC/EO/PS/11/2).

The context of the school's history can be learnt in other sources. There are several possibilities. School logbooks, complied by law by the headteacher, are not the best source for researching pupil ancestors (though they are a good source for teacher ancestors). Individuals are rarely mentioned. However, they are of interest because they note activities in the life of the school. School inspections, wartime disruption, excursions and school holidays are all mentioned. These records which are held at the LMA are closed for 100 years from date of creation, but those at THLHL&A are not subject to such restrictions.

The Bonner School logbook (held at THLHL&A) gives a good impression about the school's activities and members of staff therein. In 1898, we learn that 'Miss B. Marks absent Thursday and Friday May 12th and 13th owing to her sister ill with diphtheria'. We then learn that Beatrice Marks resided at 91 Midhurst Road, Hackney, and was not affected by her sister's illness. Children were often ill, though are never named, but the log records that for 18 days in March 1901 the school was closed due to measles, following a note that attendance was 'very low owing to many children away with measles'. Some names and addresses of pupils are occasionally given, as when ten are sent home for 'being in a dirty condition' and a few who are nominated by the medical officer as being suited for special schools. There are also remarks about repairs to the school, examinations, attendance figures, visits by the vicar and others, fire drills, Empire Day, the school being closed one afternoon 'on account of the Queen's death' and much more.

Some school archives, especially recent ones, are still held at the schools in question if they exist, so if the school archives that you seek are not at the LMA, THLHL&A, or HA, application should be made to the school in question and the council's education department. However, they may not exist or may be deemed too recent and therefore too sensitive to reveal

John Cass School, Whitechapel (photo by the author).

information to researchers unless they concern the individual making the enquiry themselves.

Many school archives no longer exist. Some were destroyed when the school was closed, others disposed of when they were no longer deemed to be of practical use for the purpose for which they were created. If you have checked all the main possibilities (LMA/HA/THLHL&A, school and education department), then you will have to conclude that this particular avenue is closed to you and you will need to look elsewhere. Schools and archive offices rarely keep exam certificates.

The following table is a summary list to the East End school archives held at the LMA. Registers from 1841 up to 1911 are searchable on the London Admissions section of Ancestry.co.uk. They are arranged chronologically by child's entry to the school, listing date of entry, date of birth, name of pupil, address, date left and comments as to destination. Please note that most of the schools listed were organised into three categories, each with its own head; Infants (aged 5–7), Boys and Girls, both aged 7–11. Each has its own set of logbooks and admission registers.

Due to space constraints the date ranges below encompass the widest date ranges of these registers so that each range does not necessarily mean that they cover all of the school's three branches. Also note that these school archives are incomplete due to records having been disposed of prior to reaching the record office.

East End school archives held at the LMA

School	Admission Books	Logbooks	Other
Alton Street, P	1887–1951	1906–34	
Atley Road, P	1872–1946	1873–1941	
Baker Street	1872–1927		
Ben Jonson		1952–78	
Berner Street, S	1872–1930	1899–1921	
Betts Street, S	1884–1933		
Bishopsgate Ward Boys	**1867–80**	**1868–89**	
Bishopsgate Ward Girls	**1863–91**	**1868–72**	
Bishop Challoner	1957–64	1958–64	
Blakesley Street, S	1891–9	1913–26	
Bonner Street	**1876–1913**	**1898–1942**	
Bow High Street, BG	1879–1932		
Bow Central School			School Magazines, 1934–7
Bow Great	**1896–1935**		
Cardinal Griffin			School Magazines, 1952–4
Cass Red Coat, S			School Magazines, 1969–73
Cayley			School Magazines, 1977–8
Central Foundation Girls	**1888–1907**		
Chatham Gardens, Sh	1875–1927	1875–1935	
Cotton Street, P	1903–6		
Cranbrook Road, BG	1877–1939	1881–1951	
Curtain Road, Sh	1886–1938	1875–1938	
Dalgleish Street, S	1880–1939	1880–1939	Visitors' Book, 1886–1906

Deal Street	1896–1939		
Elizabeth Barrett, ME	**1948–59**		
Essex Street, later John Scurr	1872–1960	1921–8	
Fairfield Road, P	1879–1946	**1876–1935**	School Magazines, 1936–46
George Yard Charity	1887–1906		
Globe Road	1874–1939	1874–1930	
Good Shepherd	**1933–55**		
Gospall Street, Sh	1931–9	1913–39	
Gravel Lane	1896–1931		
Haggerston Road, Sh	1895–1931	1879–1932	
Hague Street, BG	1883–1939	1883–1945	
Halley Street, S	1875–1936		
Hanbury Street, S	1891–1903		
Hay currie			School Magazines, **1962-1965**
John Harvard	1872–1939	1931–40	
Knapp Road, P	1883–1952	1876–1932	
Lower Chapman Street	1874–1939	1874–1930	
Maidstone Street, Sh	1868–1946	1872–1939	
Malmesbury Road, P	1885–1939	1885–1939	Honour Book, 1929–39
Marner Road	1873–1939	1893–1906	
Monteith Street, P	1881–1933	1873–1939	
Morpeth	**1943–87**		**Punishment Book, 1965–81**
Mowlem Street, BG	1887–1945	1887–1939	Honour Book, 1930-1939
Napier Street, Sh	1885–1956	1885–1939	
Northey Street, S	1893–1939		Roll of Service, 1914–1918
Oban Street, P	1883–1933	1883–1933	
Olga Street, BG	1875–1939	1874–1933	**Punishment Book, 1909–68**
Parmiter			School Magazines, 1900, **1938–80**

Pell Street, S	1903–6		
Portman Place, BG	1894–1945	1904–39	
Raine's	1736–1958	1891–1940	
Ricardo Street, P	1880–1939	1914–35	
Rochelle Street, BG	1877–1976	1914–35	
Roman Road, BG		**1913–31**	
Rutland Street,	1885–1939		
Senrab Street, S	1896–1939	1907–37	
Settley Street, S			
Shap Street, Sh	1875–1939		
Smeed Street, P	1890–1939	1885–1939	
Smith Street, S	1899–1910		
Somerford Street, BG	1889–1930	1881–1930	
St Anne's	**1886–1946**		
St Bernard's	1929-1961	**1929–50**	School Magazines, **1955–67**
St Bride's and Bridewell Precinct			
St Edmund's		1910–19	
St Ethelburgen	**1824–73**		
George Green	**1898–1913**		School Magazines, **1915–64**
St George's German Lutheran	**1828–70**		
St Mary and St Michael's		**1933–1975**	
St Matthias			School Magazines, **1934**
St Paul's Catholic		**1912–1985**	
St Philip's			School Magazines, **1979–82**
Stafford Road, P	1876-1909	1913-1924	
Stepney Greencoat	**1899–1906**	**1877–1939**	School Magazines, **1982–6**
Stepney Jewish, S	1869-1969	1884-1970	Roll of Honour, 1914–18, Medical Register, 1909–11, Punishment Book, 1939–67, **School Magazines, 1938**

Schooling and Health

Stepney Redcoat	**1912–23**		
Teesdale Street. BG	1894–1939	1873–1939	
Thomas Street,	1876–1939		
Turin Street, BG	1875–1928	1875–1929	
Twig Folly,	1878–80		
Villareal	1895–1923		
Virginia Road, BG	1875–1939	1900–43	
Wilmot Street, BG	1873–1965	1873–1965	Punishment Book, 1954–62
Wilton Road, Sh	1886–1926	1912–1937	
Wolverley Street, BG	1873–1938	1877–1938	
Wood Close	**1920–47**		
Woolmore Street, P	1882–1939	1876–1939	
Wrights Road		1877–1891	

BG means Bethnal Green, ME is Mile End, P stands for Poplar, S for Stepney and Sh for Shoreditch. Archives listed above are held at the LMA; from 1840-1911 they must be viewed on Ancestry.co.uk; thereafter, for the registers on microfilm. Items in **bold** are held at THLHL&A. THLHL&A's admission registers prior to 1911 can be seen at FindMyPast.co.uk.

The LMA also holds a great deal more about the educational history of the East End. This includes photographs and plans of schools, as well as committee minute books about the establishment and managing of the schools in question.

Events in schools were widely reported in the press, especially on their being opened by civic dignitaries. These articles describe the school as it was when it opened.

When we think of the East End we do not often think of private schools. Yet in the nineteenth century a great many existed throughout London, including the East End. These were often very small and did not last long, closing when the proprietor died or retired and so few records exist. However, these schools advertised and the local press is a good place to find out about your ancestors be they teachers or pupils at these schools, as indicated from the census returns or directories. The following is an advert from the *East London Observer* of 3 April 1869:

EAST LONDON
> Collegiate School for Ladies
> 42 Burdett Road E
> (Corner of Clemence Street)
>
> UNDER THE PATRONAGE OF
> The Rev. Canon CHAMPREYS, MA
> The Rev. Canon DALE, MA
> And several other Clergymen & Ladies
>
> THE SCHOOL COURSE
>
> Comprises of a thorough English Education, with French, German, Class Singing, Calisthenics, Needlework, &c. The thoroughness of the education is proved by the fact that, although the school has not yet been opened two years, two pupils passed as seniors at the recent Cambridge Local Examinations. No other school at the East End of London has passed any pupils. The year is divided into three terms. Fees for pupils under nine years of age, three guineas per annum. Pupils under twelve years of age six guineas per annum. Pupils above twelve years of age nine guineas per annum. Music one guinea or one and a half guineas per term. Solo singing £1 8s per term. Boarders 30, 33 and 36 guineas per annum, according to age.

How accurate this information is is one question, and how much has been omitted is another, for this is an advert designed to encourage parents to pay for their daughters to be schooled here. Yet it is a unique source of evidence for this East End school.

School archives are not only informative about the schools and the pupils, but about the teachers, too. If you have a teacher amongst your ancestors, then the school logbooks and other archives (governors' and managers' minute books for example) are an excellent source of information about them. In fact, logbooks are more informative about teachers than they are about pupils as teachers are routinely mentioned for a variety of reasons. These include information about teachers being appointed, starting work, being off school (due to sickness and family bereavements or due to enlisting in wartime), taking pupils on excursions and so on.

Walter Besant complained about the lack of a reading culture in the East End in the nineteenth century, but he did emphasise the work of two newly established institutions there. Higher and adult education came to the East End at the end of the nineteenth century in the form of the

The London Hospital, Whitechapel (collection of John Coulter).

lectures held at the People's Palace Technical School, established on Mile End Road in 1887 and opened by the Queen, and at Toynbee Hall on Commercial Street; some annual reports and works on the latter can be found at THLHL&A (A/TOY). The People's Palace and the East End Technical College merged to become the Queen Mary College, which in 1934 became part of the University of London. Annual Reports from 1954 to 1982, prospectuses 1967–85 and calendars 1958–70 can be viewed at THLHL&A. Archives of these organisations exist at the LMA and parent bodies.

Hospitals

Health in the East End was a major concern. Smoking and drinking were almost universal. Homes were very smoky because of this and the atmosphere generally was poor because of coal-burning fires. Respiratory problems were caused by both industrial and domestic pollution. Simon Webb wrote 'This smoky atmosphere in the home was one reason for the high incidence of bronchitis among children from working class districts' (middle-class households used gas rather than coal). Webb described his hospital experiences in the 1960s at Queen Elizabeth Hospital, Hackney Road:

> It was a grim Victorian building ... I spent a fortnight in the Queen Elizabeth Hospital in 1961 and it was one of the most miserable times of my life. Not that the staff were cruel or neglectful, they were anything but that. But things were pretty regimented and the emphasis was far more on cleanliness and order than it was on making homesick children feel a bit better ... There was no doubt at all as to whom was important in these wards; it was the doctors and matrons.

Jennifer Worth's three volumes of memoirs as a midwife in Poplar in the 1950s – *Call the Midwife*, *Eczema and Food Allergy* and *Shadows of the Workhouse* – also portray medical life from the point of view of the midwives there, but provide vignettes of life of those they came in contact with.

The major hospitals in the East End were as follows:

1. London Hospital, Whitechapel Road, was founded in 1759. In the early twentieth century it had accommodation for nearly 1,000 inpatients. Patient records for 1760–1991, registers of sisters and nurses from 1880 to 1946 and staff salaries for 1742–1958 and much more can be found at the Royal London Hospital Archives Centre and Museum.
2. Bethnal Green Hospital, Cambridge Heath Road, E1, 1962–74 (H21): Children's Registers, 1891–1918; History of children, 1896–1906. Held at the LMA.
3. East End Maternity Hospital, Commercial Road, E1, 1884–1969 (held at the Royal London Hospital Archives Centre and Museum): Patient records, 1884–1968, register of midwife pupils, 1924–41, register of midwives, 1899–1916, register of trainee midwives, 1924–41.
4. Hoxton Street Infirmary (SHBG, 145–50): Records include registers of patient admission and discharges, 1872–1902, creed registers, 1851–1905, death registers 1872–85, register of male patients, 1876–1906, registers of female patients, 1872–1910, and a register of the friends of patients, 1890–1. Held at the LMA.

5. Metropolitan Hospital, Commercial Street, Spitalfields (1876–86) and at Kingsland Road, Shoreditch (1886–1977): Records include registers of patient admissions, 1923–46, registers of births, 1909–65, registers of deaths, 1963–75 and clinical records, 1927–77. Held at the LMA.
6. Mile End Hospital, Bancroft Road, E1, 1844–1952 (H21/ME): Creed Registers, 1919–33, Nurses' Certificate Books, 1911–32, Mortuary Registers, 1936–46, Nursery Admissions Registers, 1930–6. Held at the LMA.
7. St Leonard's Hospital, Nuttall Street, Shoreditch, 1879–1986 (H19): Records include admission registers, 1898–1967, registers of births, 1892–1938, registers of deaths, 1885–1969, case notes, 1907–13 and 1937–48. Held at the LMA.
8. Whitechapel Infirmary, later St Peter's Hospital (SRBG/WH/123): Records include registers of patient admission and discharges, 1853–1925 (indexed 1900–17), creed registers, 1910–26, birth registers, 1902–25, death registers 1877–1916, and a register of the friends of patients, 1868–1911. Held at the LMA.

People's Palace, Mile End Road (collection of John Coulter).

Patient registers list patients and brief details of the treatment, with date. Arranged chronologically, these records are not indexed by name and are closed for 100 years except to the data subject.

Creed registers are similar to those in the archives of workhouses. They list, in chronological order, name, age, date of admission, creed (although some are listed as Catholic or Jewish the overwhelming majority are listed as Church of England; the standard default position of many agnostics and atheists, then; unlike the 2001 census, declaring oneself to be a Jedi was not an option) and date of discharge or death. An example from the Mile End creed register is of Mary A. Atkinson, aged 66, admitted on 14 July 1919, Church of England; died 14 October 1919.

Nursery admission and discharge registers give similar information; date of admission, name, sex, age, calling if applicable, creed, name and address of next of kin, classification, date of discharge and destination. So, for Thursday 21 August 1930, June Agnes Oldfield, female, aged 2 years and 7 months, Church of England, mother Matilda Oldfield of 58 Royal Mint Street, was admitted to Mile End Hospital.

Health

Since the outbreaks of cholera and typhus which killed thousands of Londoners in the early nineteenth century, public health has been of major concern to government. Local government districts, since 1856, employed a doctor to be their Medical Officer of Health, who had to investigate cases of ill health in the district, to make recommendations for action and to compile statistics of cases of ill health and reasons for deaths, giving numbers of deaths by cause. His reports were published annually and give a good overview of the health or otherwise of a district. There would also be comments on matters which might affect an area's health – changes in transport, building operations, open spaces. Many of these reports (e.g. Shoreditch, 1886–1964, Poplar, 1894–1965, Stepney, 1901–65, Whitechapel, 1856–1901) can be found on the website of the Wellcome Institute for the History of Medicine, www.wellcomelibrary.org/moh/about-the-reports/about-the-medical-officer-of-health-reports. They do not list individuals, but they do tell how common certain illnesses and disease were.

For example, the Whitechapel Medical Officer of Health's Annual Report for 1888 provides a wealth of statistical data about the district's health. There are estimates of population divided by the different districts which comprise the area for recent years as well as 1888. We learn that, in 1888, 25.2 per cent of all deaths were of those aged under one year and that a further 15.8 per cent of all mortality occurred to children from one to five years. While we may feel that these figures are grim, comprising as they do 41 per cent of all who died in Whitechapel in 1888, the author of the report stated that this was an improvement, because in the previous year the figure had been 44.9 per cent.

There are figures for the causes of deaths, broken down by type, age range and sex per quarter of the year. Overall, 1,574 people died; 57 from measles, 40 from scarlet fever, 54 from dysentery and diarrhoea, 59 from venereal disease and so on. There were 265 inquests. The report also referred to the Jack the Ripper murders (murder being the cause of 0.44 per cent of all deaths that year in Whitechapel). Apparently, the killer 'without doubt was a lunatic. It is also clear to those who are familiar with the district, that were the miscreant a resident in the district, he could not have escaped detection.' The medical officer was annoyed that many people credited Whitechapel residents with all killings in the East

Toynbee Hall, Whitechapel, 1885 (collection of Lindsay Siviter).

End, pointing out that in 1862–88 there had been but 29 murders in Whitechapel and of these, six were infanticides and five were the Ripper's work.

Apart from deaths, there are figures for the number of births in the district, broken down by quarter, district and sex. Numbers of inmates entering the workhouse and the hospital were also provided. On average nearly 300 people came to the former every week and nearly 70 went into hospital per week. A summary of the work of the health department was also provided; inspections of domestic and work premises, issuing notices for necessary improvements and carrying out tests to determine the safety of foodstuffs and other consumable items.

There was a smallpox vaccination campaign in Shoreditch in the early twentieth century and records were kept of this public health initiative. At HA are the vaccination registers, 1904–18 (S/R/1/1–32). These list the name of the child, date of birth and date of vaccination.

Chapter 10

GENERAL SOURCES

There are numerous other sources which will be useful for family and local historians that have not been fully – if at all – discussed so far.

Maps

Probably the best way to see where your ancestors lived is to use maps. There are many series of maps which are of value. Maps of London and Middlesex exist from the sixteenth century to date. There is the Agas map of about 1561 at the LMA, which is the earliest printed map of the capital. More a view with illustrations than a map proper, it covers the western parts of the East End.

There is a map of southern Shoreditch of 1559 at HA. An eighteenth-century map of Shoreditch is that of Peter Chassereau, held at HA. More comprehensive coverage of London and its environs can be seen on the John Rocque maps of 1741–5 and later editions depict London and its environs, about ten miles from the capital's centre. These do not show the majority of individual buildings. They name streets and show features such as fields and rivers. In the 1840s there are the tithe maps, showing individual properties, together with associated apportionments with details of land usage, acreage and names of owners and tenants. The 1703 Gascoyne map covers Stepney and is useful.

The most important set of maps are the Ordnance Survey maps which cover 1865 to the 1970s. Produced every two decades in paper format, they show each building and street, with prominent public and private buildings (churches, town halls, docks, warehouses, large houses) named.

Natural geographical features are depicted, as is altitude. There is also a myriad of abbreviations to denote other places of note, such as pubs and post boxes. Up to the Second World War houses are rarely numbered, but afterwards they are. The earlier maps, up to 1936 are 25 inches on the map to a mile in reality and another series of 60 inches to the mile; afterwards they are 50 inches to a mile. There are also the inner London OS maps series which are five feet to the mile and the most detailed maps available from the 1860s to the 1930s.

OS maps are, by their nature, large and bulky, and so best seen flat on a table indoors. However, many of these maps can be purchased commercially from Alan Godfrey Maps (www.alangodfreymaps.co.uk). They are smaller in size than the originals, but can be folded up and are ideal for walking a district in order to make comparisons with what is on the ground now and so find the location of a long-vanished series of houses or a factory now no more. A list of what is available can be found on the company's website. Currently there are maps of all of the East End from the mid-Victorian era to the Edwardian age: Shoreditch (1872, 1893, 1914), Bethnal Green (1870, 1894, 1914), Bromley and Bow (1867, 1893, 1914), Whitechapel (1873, 1894, 1913), Stepney (1870, 1914) and Poplar (1867, 1894, 1914).

There are numerous other maps, some being one-offs. The Charles Booth Poverty map, created between 1886 and 1903, should be of great interest, for it shows London, street by street. Each street is coloured; from gold to show great affluence to black to indicate great poverty. In between are different shades of reds and blues. The map can be seen online at www.booth.lse.ac.uk. There is a 1935 geological survey which includes Shoreditch at HA. Borough councils commissioned maps of the borough, often to use for electoral purposes or for building projects and THLHL&A has a number for the early to mid-twentieth century.

Map collections can be seen at both HA and THLHL&A, as well as at the British Library Map Room and TNA. HA has copies of the five 60 inch to the mile (1:1056) OS maps from 1868-1934, four editions of the 25 inch to a mile OS maps for the same date spans, a copy of the 6 inch to the mile 1935 edition and copies of the post-1945 50 inch to a mile (1:1250) editions. Maps less than 50 years old can be photocopied in their entirety.

A number of maps can be seen at the Digital Resource section of the THLHL&A website (https://www.ideastore.co.uk/assets/documents/

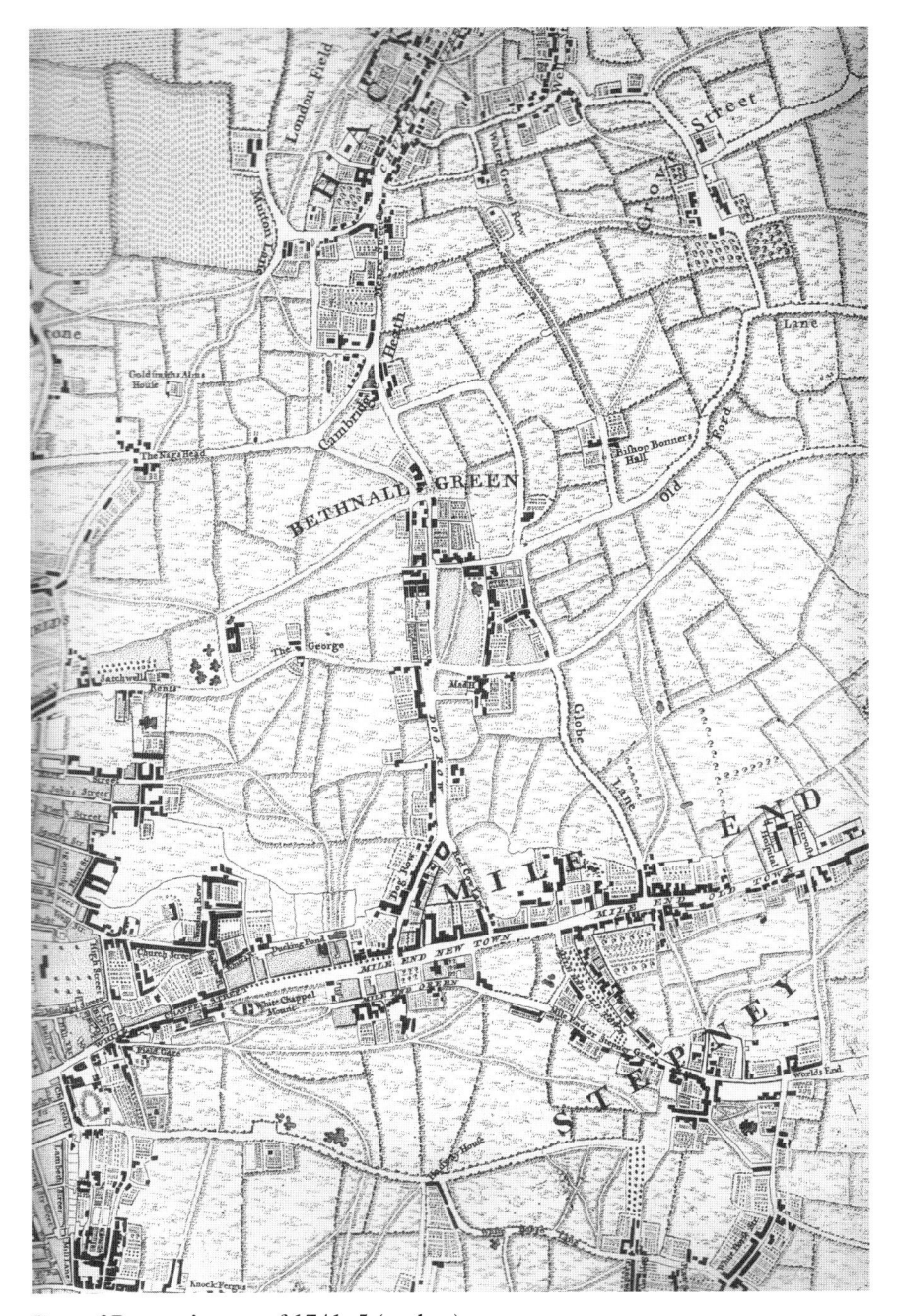

Part of Rocque's map of 1741–5 (author).

Local%20History%20Archives%20Online/user%20guides/maps%20v4%20(8%20pages)%20FINAL.pdf). These include maps dating from 1827, 1832 and 1862–71 amongst others. Other online maps can be seen on the East London History Society website's Map Gallery. This features a greater range of maps, dating from 1703 to 2000, but excludes Ordnance Survey maps. Others can be seen at www.oldmaps.co.uk and at http://maps.nls.uk/series.

Photographs

One of the most popular sources for local history, to the extent that there exist whole books of them, together with additional information, is old photographs. Since the dawn of the photographic age in the mid-nineteenth century, this relatively quick and inexpensive (compared to paintings) way of recording scenes from real life has proved enduringly popular. The wealth of information that can be captured on a photograph varies considerably, depending on the scene. If people and transport as well as a built environment are included then its value as a social record is greater still, as well as being more intrinsically interesting.

Photography was a rich man's hobby at first, though there were professional photographers, and it increasingly became a middle-class interest until the later twentieth century. One offshoot of the photography businesses which developed in the early twentieth century, and was at its height from about 1900 to 1920, was the postcard industry. Although designed as a cheap and effective form of communication, it also served to create mini works of art which, like photographs, are now snapshots of a long gone age.

However, photographers and postcard makers were primarily businessmen not social historians. They focused on parts of London which would be popular and attractive to the perceived consumers, so pictures of well-known landmarks and prosperous districts were more common than postcards of less well off parts of the capital where locals would be less likely to purchase postcards. There are a few postcards of the East End, of course. These include the famous Petticoat Market, the London Hospital, the docks and several of the prominent churches.

The Hackney on disc database allows access to the photograph collection as digitised copies via keyword searches. A selection of the

36,000 photographs from the THLHL&A collection can be viewed online on their Digital Gallery. It is possible to search the collection by location and by decade, and also by subject matter (the latter including subjects such as parks, pubs, strikes and women). The East London History Society's Picture Gallery on their website also features a large variety of historic pictures; comic postcards of the East End, East End greetings cards, pictures of East End markets, Victorian portraits of East-enders, pictures of the construction of the Olympic Stadium and old photographs contributed by the society's members.

Paintings and Prints

Prior to photographs there were other illustrations, though these were relatively rare because of the time and expense needed to create just one. However, until the mid–nineteenth century they are the only form of pictorial record of a place. Oil paintings in the THLHL&A collection can be viewed on the BBC Your Paintings website, www.bbc.co.uk/arts/yourpaintings/paintings/search and can then be searched by place.

Audio-Visual

Pictures are good, but they are by definition two dimensional and static. Moving pictures and sound add an extra dimension and make the past more real. HA has 50 films and videos, one being of Hoxton and Shoreditch from the 1920s.

Directories

Directories are predominantly nineteenth- and twentieth-century listings of people and businesses in a particular geographical location and so are useful for tracing people between the censuses. However, unlike the largely middle-class parts of London and much of the provinces, there are only a few street directories specifically for the East End, covering Stratford, Bow and Mile End, 1866; Poplar, Limehouse and Stepney, 1866; Bow, Bromley and Old Field, 1867; Bethnal Green, 1872 and 1888. All can be seen at THLHL&A. There are none specifically for Shoreditch. London directories include the East End, though very few of the Middlesex directories (none after about 1826) do, despite the East End being part of that county until 1889.

These general London trades directories were produced by such businesses as Pigot's in the early nineteenth century. From the middle of the nineteenth century to the late twentieth, these directories were produced by Kelly's. They were divided into a number of sections. These were an alphabetical listing of all London streets, often naming shops and prominent residents for each. Then there is an alphabetical list of private residents, but this is only a very limited list of householders, mostly the well to do. Thirdly there is the Commercial and Professional section, a list of businesses in alphabetical order and finally the Trades and Professional section, which lists these by type of business and then alphabetically.

When a series of directories exist, as they do for the twentieth century, they allow the history of a street and/or district to be studied. Businesses come and go, they expand and decline and the directories, which list them and their whereabouts, are a great source to trace their existence. Some London directories can be seen online, at http://specialcollections.le.ac.uk/cdm/landingpage/collection/p16445coll4. At HA there are early London directories from 1677, 1760 and 1777, then others form an incomplete run from 1804 to 1986. THLHL&A has London directories from 1790 to the 1980s (some gaps) with others from 1667 to 1889 on microfilm. LMA and the Guildhall Library also hold extensive collections of directories. These directories, unlike electoral registers, continued to be published during the Second World War.

It should be noted that the streets in the East End have often been renamed over the decades, as has occurred elsewhere in London. In order to locate streets which are no longer marked on modern maps, you should consult the gazetteer of London streets created in 1955 (there are also earlier editions of 1901, 1912 and 1928) which lists streets in existence then and street names that they replaced. There is also a list of streets which have since been renamed in the back of the book. Both are in alphabetical order and so names can be easily found.

We could add that there are also the London telephone directories from 1880, but very few people, even businesses, in the East End, had telephones installed until the middle of the twentieth century. For those few which did, they can be searched on Ancestry.co.uk from 1880 to 1984.

Part of Stanford's map of London, 1911 (author).

Guidebooks and Contemporary Histories

London has always attracted numerous visitors from home and abroad. In the nineteenth and twentieth centuries, this has led to books being written for the benefit of the tourist, both foreign and homegrown. They give the reader information that would be well known to a resident of any district described, so is invaluable to the researcher who is akin to a visitor in a foreign country. However, inevitably these books, as with postcards, focus on the parts of London which are generally of more interest to the sightseer, and that means the West End not the East End.

Yet they do not neglect our district wholly. To take *Bradshaw's Illustrated Hand Book to London and its environs* (1862), there are ten pages devoted to the 'East' and over 50 to both the West and the City, with 24 to the north and 14 to the south, as well as additional chapters for Windsor, Greenwich and Gravesend. There is also a 15-page guide to the Thames. The book envisages that the visitor is to take several days visiting the different parts of the capital.

The chapter on the East begins thus, 'The eastern division of London will be found to present a marked contrast to the other portions of the metropolis'. There follow descriptions of the numerous docks: St Katharine's, London and the West Indies. Apart from descriptions of the docks and commercial information, there is social commentary, too:

> Along the quay you see, now men with their faces blue with indigo, and now gaugers with their long brass tipped rule dripping with spirit from the cask they have been probing; then come a group of flaxen-haired sailors, chattering German, and next a black sailor with a cotton handkerchief twisted turban-like around his head.

Parts of it are rather dismissive of the districts, for example, 'Whitechapel has nothing but the butchers' shambles to boast of as a characteristic feature. The church has no features of architectural or historical interest'. The houses in Bethnal Green are 'generally miserably small and densely inhabited … this squalid region'. Shoreditch had an 'uninviting appearance'. However, he makes favourable remarks about Victoria Park, the gourmet treats of Blackwall and the new Greek church.

Contemporary histories of London are also of interest, combining observations on local history as well as contemporary topography. Generally speaking, the latter is of more interest to the current reader, though its middle-class bias should be noted.

Records of Local Government

Both HA and THLHL&A hold many of the core records of their parent bodies especially from the nineteenth and twentieth centuries. These are the minute books of the various local government bodies; minute books of the full council and committee minute books for the myriad number of committees. These include those for Baths, Highways, Housing and

Public Libraries, to name but four. Up to the mid-nineteenth century the parish was the font of local government, followed by the local boards from 1855 to 1900, then the metropolitan boroughs up to 1965. Some of the boroughs were essentially continuations of the local boards, as with Shoreditch, but in some cases they merged, as with Whitechapel becoming part of Stepney. These archives are useful for the local historian in ascertaining how local government responded to local issues, but bear in mind that the LCC, from 1889, had powers over education and housing in the East End, so these records (at the LMA) should be consulted, too, depending on the research topic.

Tax Records

The Hearth Tax was introduced in 1662 after the restoration of the Stuart monarchy in 1660 and abolished with the revolution of 1688. It was a direct form of taxation imposed by central government on properties; a set amount being levied on each hearth, so larger properties had a larger bill. The entire records for the London and Middlesex Hearth Tax were published by the British Records Society in 2014 in a two-volume book format. Those for 1666 alone can be seen on www.hearthtax.org.uk. The original records can also be seen at TNA in class E179.

It was replaced by the Land Tax. Records are organised by county and list taxpayer and amount assessed for. The lists for the following East End parishes can be found at LMA: Bethnal Green (1829–1930), Bow (1747–66), Bromley St Leonard's (1783–1926), Limehouse (1732–1825), Mile End (1741–1930), Poplar (1743–1815), Ratclif (1730–1828), St George in the East (1730–1823), Shoreditch (1806–1923), Shadwell (1731–1917), Spitalfields (1743–1923), Wapping (1730–1826) and Whitechapel (1733–1922). Land Tax records up to 1832 can be viewed at Ancestry.co.uk. Copies of some of these for Poplar, Bow and Bromley and Bethnal Green can be found at THLHL&A.

The importance of such tax records to the genealogist is that they can show how wealthy an individual was and where they owned property. For the local historian they can provide a snapshot of the distribution of property and wealth in any given parish, and who had what. When a number of such returns exist, these can show how fortunes change, or not, over a period of time. For the Hearth Tax, the records can give an indication of population, and its fluctuations, especially how it changed due to the impact of the great plague of 1665, though burial registers should also be used in conjunction with them.

Rating Records

The borough councils followed the example of the parishes in levying rates for their increasing expenditure in the twentieth century. The books list properties (this time with a complete street address), name of ratepayer and amount levied, based on property size. They were produced annually (unlike electoral registers which went unpublished during 1940–4):

1. Bethnal Green, 1959–64 (L/BGM/C/45, 11, 17, 23, 29) – at THLHL&A
2. Stepney, 1959–64 (L/SMB/C/2/4/14, 30, 46, 62, 77) – at THLHL&A
3. Shoreditch, 1901–65 (S/FRR) – at HA.

Census Returns

The census returns of 1841–1911 are well known to the researcher as a most valuable source, but a number of censuses held prior to the former year did include names. Those for the East End are the 1821 and 1831 returns for Poplar, which can be seen at THLHL&A (L/ASP/E/9/1–4).

These generally give less information than those for 1851 onwards, merely listing householders and household size. Yet if you have a Poplar ancestor, this will enable you to pinpoint him in the parish at that time. For example, we learn that John Johnson, in 1831, lived in a household of eight males and four females. We know how many of each sex was in various age categories and in which employment designation (agriculture, trade or other). At the book's end there is a summary of how many in the parish were engaged in each, a list of streets, number of houses, occupied, unoccupied or in process of being built.

Poll Books and Electoral Registers

Poll books for Middlesex cover that minority of adult male voters for the East End. They were only produced on the occasion of an election but do list who the voters voted for; as this was a county constituency returning two members to Parliament, each voter could cast two votes. Poll Books for the county of Middlesex survive for 1749/50, 1768/9, 1802 and 1806 at the LMA. Following the Reform Act of 1832, new constituencies were created, one being that of the one-member constituency of Shoreditch and relevant poll books for 1843 and 1845 can be seen at HA. Another new constituency which covered other parts of the East End was Tower Hamlets. Poll books for this one for 1832, 1833, 1834/5–1837/8, 1839/40–1854/5, 1856–1865/6 and 1883–5 are to be found at the LMA.

There are also parochial returns of those eligible to vote, with names and addresses, as created by the parish overseers. Those which can be viewed on Ancestry.co.uk are as follows: Bethnal Green, 1864, 1867, Bromley, 1863, 1864, 1885–7, Spitalfields, 1882, 1885–7, Mile End New Town, 1863–5, Mile End Hamlet, 1863–4, Mile End Old Town, 1863–4, 1885–7, Ratcliff, 1863–4, 1885–7, Limehouse, 1863–4, 1885–7, Wapping, 1863–4, 1885–7, Shadwell, 1863–4, 1885–7, Whitechapel, 1963, Stratford, 1863–4, 1885–7, St George in the East, 1863, 1885–7 and Shoreditch, 1863–4, 1885–7.

From 1872 electoral registers were produced annually except in 1916–17 and 1940–4. With the Secret Ballot Act of 1872, there was now no way of knowing who had voted for whom, reducing bribery and corruption but also reducing the amount of information available to the genealogist. These are not indexed by name but by street. Up to 1918, franchise was granted to householders (male and female (from 1885) – usually widows, but including some unmarried females). From 1918 to 1927 men aged 21 or over could vote and women aged 30 or over; from 1928 to 1969 everyone aged 21 or over could vote; from 1969 18 was the minimum voting age. Note that those of foreign nationality (except people from the Commonwealth) cannot vote and so are excluded from these registers, though some immigrants became naturalised and so can vote.

Electoral Registers for Shoreditch for 1879, 1897–1964 can be viewed at HA. From 1965 the registers are included in those for the London Borough of Hackney and these, from 1965 onwards, can also be seen at HA. Some can be seen on Ancestry.co.uk. Type Electoral Registers into the Card Catalogue section, select London Electoral Registers, 1832–1965, then pick Shoreditch and the year that you want to check first. Those which can be searched thus by name are those for the years 1880, 1885–7, 1889, 1914–15, 1919–21 and 1961–2.

The LMA holds electoral registers for Tower Hamlets for 1873–89 and for Bethnal Green for 1885–9 and then for all of what is now Tower Hamlets from 1890 onwards. At THLHL&A can be seen the registers for Tower Hamlets, which included Poplar and Stepney (1901–14), Bethnal Green (1901–64), Poplar (1918–64), Stepney (1918–64) and from 1965 to 2002 for the newly created London Borough of Tower Hamlets. A few can be seen on Ancestry.co.uk: Bethnal Green, 1962–3, Poplar, 1962–3 and Stepney, 1961–3.

Electoral registers are useful for ascertaining how long families were resident at particular addresses and when members left the main family abode. Local historians can use them for ascertaining when houses and streets were first in occupancy, usually equating to when they were built, and when or if they were demolished, for then the streets/houses will no longer appear in the listings. They also indicate premises which were in multiple occupancy as many houses often were, as can be noted when a number of couples/families are listed in a particular property. They are also useful for tracing the local history of immigration, for they will show when particular streets/districts became increasingly occupied by people from overseas and when families have departed the locality.

Protestation Rolls

In 1642, at the onset of civil war, a survey was made of each parish to discover political loyalties and thus lists of male householders were created and kept. These rolls will tell who was resident in a particular parish. It will also give a rough indication of the local population at that time. The originals are housed at the Parliamentary Archives (HL/PO/JO/10/1/99). For the East End they exist for Shoreditch, Bow, Bromley and Stepney and hamlets.

Manorial Records

Manors were territorial units held by a landlord, lay or clerical, in which tenants worked on the land and paid rents to the landlord. They were only formally abolished in 1925, but had been in decline for centuries before then. Prior to the parish registers, the best source of names is the manorial records. These were accounts of meetings of the manorial courts, which met regularly to decide on business relevant to the manor (a unit of landholding). These included inheritance, rent and services payable to the lord, damage to property and minor crimes. Manorial records for Stepney exist from 1189 to 1925 and can be found at the LMA, TNA, THLHL&A (L/SMB/G/1) and the British Library. These include court books from 1654 to 1925, surveys of the manor, accounts, rentals, lists of juries and rents. Poplar manor's records from 1889 to 1925 are held at TNA and THLHL&A (P/PLC), including court books, rentals, court rolls and estreats. These often give our only insight into local life and local events in the Middle Ages and beyond, so anyone interested in a district's medieval history cannot ignore them.

Land Values Books

In 1910, a survey of all property in Britain was undertaken for taxation purposes. So comprehensive was this survey that it is sometimes referred to as the Domesday survey after that of William I in 1086. However, it is far more detailed and thus useful than that from Norman times. Books were written up for each parish, listing each property, together with owner, tenant (if different), rateable value and perhaps other details. These books are to be found at THLHL&A and HA for the appropriate parts of the East End. Maps and related material can be found at TNA.

Deeds

When private land changes hands legally, documents have to be drawn up by lawyers to complete the transaction. These show the names of those selling/renting the property, those who are buying/renting it, what the property is, giving details of buildings, fields and other resources there, often with acreage, its location in relation to other properties adjoining, such as roads, houses and fields, how much the purchase price or rent is, and any other condition, i.e. in tenancies that trees are not to be lopped or stipulations that any property built on land bought is not to be used for certain commercial purposes. Deeds, where they survive, and thousands do, are held at THLHL&A, LMA and HA and can be located by searching their online catalogues, by name of property or by seller/buyer, so anyone with an ancestor who sold/bought/leased or rented property might well find them here. Not all do still exist, however. They may also include plans of the property in question. Until 1733 deeds are written in Latin. Yet for 1733–1889, there is the Middlesex Registry of Deeds at the LMA, which is a huge collection of the abstracts of all deeds enrolled with the county quarter sessions (the registry continued until the 1930s but only covered the county of Middlesex and by 1889 the East End had become part of the county of London). However, they are indexed by year and then by the party selling/renting, not by property name. Often many exist for the same property and may cover decades or even centuries.

As an example of the description of a property which changed hands, on 22 February 1850, Charles Hunter rented this to John Wheen for an annual rent of £150 (THLHL&A, B/MIS/35):

> all that freehold messuage dwelling house or tenement situate and being in old Gravel Lane, Ratcliff Highway in the county of Middlesex together with the yard, gardens, stables, buildings and appurtenances thereto belonging situate and being in old Gravel Lane aforesaid and near or adjoining the said messuage together also with a courtway entrance or road leading to Ratcliff Highway for the said premises which said messuage buildings and premises are used as a soap premises which said messuage buildings and premises are used as a soap manufactory formerly in the possession of Messieurs WH Sharp and John Bland Hanbury and are now in care of the said John Wheen.

Deeds are important for both local and family historians. For the former, they help show how a locality changed over time, who the builders were, and if land is being used for building purposes as much was in the nineteenth century. Family historians will be interested in the names that appear in the deeds if they are those of their propertied ancestors, as it will give additional evidence about their activities.

Newspapers

The local press was at its best from the middle of the nineteenth century to the later twentieth. It contained personal announcements of births, marriages and deaths (paid for, so usually of the middle classes). Inquests were often reported, as were sporting (especially football and cricket when in season), crime and social events. Local politics and the meetings of public bodies were reported in great detail.

Local newspapers for the East End are as follows: *East London Advertiser*, 1866–date, *East End Observer*, 1857–1914, *East End News*, 1869–1963, the *Eastern Argus*, 1877–1912, the *Hackney Express and Shoreditch Observer*, 1857–79, renamed *Hackney Express*, 1883–1903, then *Shoreditch Observer*, 1904–15. These can be seen at THLHL&A on microfilm; the latter at HA. HA has news cuttings related to Shoreditch for 1893 and 1895–1965. Remember that eighteenth- and nineteenth-century national newspapers may also feature stories from the East End, and a search on the subscription site British Newspaper Archive could well pay dividends. THLHL&A and HA also hold newspaper cuttings files relevant for their locales, too. THLHL&A's is extremely extensive. Newspaper holdings at THLHL&A can be checked at http://www.ideasstore.co.uk/assets/documents/Local%History%20Newspapers.pdf.

Local historians must pay attention to the local press of the district that they are interested in. It will often publish information that might appear nowhere else. The letters pages and editorials give local opinions on public matters, both locally, nationally and internationally, recording voices which may not be found anywhere else. The newspapers provide lengthy reports of council meetings, especially in the nineteenth and early twentieth centuries.

There are other written sources; collections of ephemera, for instance, pamphlets and much more, which can be found by checking HA's and THLHL&A's online catalogue. The issue is knowing when to stop researching and a lot will depend on time and the researcher's devotion to the topic.

Chapter 11

PLACES TO SEE AND VISIT

Although much research can be carried out online, there are still places that it will be physically useful to visit to undertake your research, and many of the items already mentioned in this book can only be seen in their original format or on microfilm in these places. The major ones are as follows.

The National Archives

Initially founded as the Public Record Office at Chancery Lane in 1838, this was the place for the storage of the archives of central government once they have been transferred from the departments of state who created them in the first place. These include those of the War Office, Admiralty, Metropolitan Police, Home Office and so on. The records from this location were all finally moved to a new site at Kew by 1996, which was renamed the National Archives in 2002. Apart from these records there is a good reference library and numerous databases which are free to access (including Ancestry.co.uk and other genealogical sites, principally FindmyPast).

Access to archives is only by a reader's ticket, available freely with proofs of identity. You will also need to see an online guide to document handling. Up to 12 archives can be ordered in advance of your visit; thereafter a maximum of three may be ordered at any one time.

Located at Ruskin Avenue, Kew, Surrey TW9 4DU
Tel. 020 8876 3444
Website: www.nationalarchives.gov.uk

London Metropolitan Archives, 2017 (photo taken by the author).

Opening hours: Wednesday, Friday and Saturday, 9-5, Tuesday and Thursday, 9-7. Closed on Sunday and Monday.

TNA's website includes numerous guides to sources held there as well as a searchable catalogue, Discovery, and numerous records available online. The catalogue enables a researcher to search the catalogues of other archives as well as TNA, so you may wish to choose the option of material held at TNA only, and then you can limit the search by both date and/or government department or at a specified repository.

The London Metropolitan Archives

This was originally the Middlesex Record Office and was the county record office for Middlesex and the LCC Record Office for London – mirroring county record offices which existed in other counties in England from the 1930s to the 1970s. It was renamed the Greater London Record Office in 1979, following the amalgamation of the Middlesex and London record offices and has been called the London Metropolitan Archives since 1997. It was crucially established before the boroughs of Greater London were recognised as places for archival deposit, which is why so many parish and school records are held here, but also because the

LCC was the administrative body for schools. Between 2005 and 2010 the archives of the Corporation of London and those archives held at the Guildhall Library were brought together at the LMA.

It collects material on a London-wide basis; in particular items of London-wide bodies such as the former county councils of Middlesex, London (1889–1965) and Greater London (1965–86), the Middlesex Quarter Sessions (1549–1971) and the Metropolitan Board of Works (1855–89), as well as the archives of London and Middlesex churches and other places of religion, courts, prisons and schools. It also possesses a good library of books on London history which are on open access.

Access to archives here is by possession of a History Card, which can be acquired by showing proofs of identity. You will need to bring this on subsequent visits. To ascertain what there is, and to note the appropriate reference number, you can either check the paper lists or the computer catalogues (you may wish to do this online prior to a visit). You can order six items at a time by completing a short form per document and putting the slips into a box on the staff desk. These are collected at set times per day (about every half an hour). Expect to wait a further 30 minutes for the documents to arrive and then to read one at a time. It is worth ordering additional items once your first batch has been collected.

Located at 40 Northampton Road, London EC1R 0HB
Tel. 020 7332 3820
Website: www.cityoflondon.gov.uk/lma
Email address: ask.LMA@corpoflondon.gov.uk

Opening hours: Mondays, 9.30–4.45, Tuesday, Wednesday, Thursday and Friday, 9.30–7.30, one Saturday per month, 9.30–4.45.

The website for LMA includes numerous information sheets for many aspects of London's history and family history, divided by themes, so are well worth reading. There is also the catalogue of LMA's archives, which you can search. The catalogue is arguably designed for archivists by archivists in that it is hierarchical, with levels from collection level to series level to item level and so it is often necessary to click on a level down in order to see listings of individual items, e.g. logbooks or admission registers for schools.

Tower Hamlets Archives (photo taken by the author, 2017).

Tower Hamlets Local History and Archives

All London boroughs collect archives and local history material pertaining to the local history of that borough and its predecessor boroughs (including archives of the borough and its predecessor local authorities and organisations, books, maps, newspapers, photographs and pictures). These are usually part of the library service for that borough. The most important local authority archive for East End research is that covering the London Borough of Tower Hamlets. Although the building's exterior looks forbidding, the interior and the helpful and knowledgeable staff inside make a visit most rewarding.

Readers must register with the service on their first visit, by bringing proof of identity.

Opening hours: Tuesday, 10–5, Wednesday and Saturday (first and third in month only), 9–5, Thursday, 9–8. Closed on Sunday, Monday and Friday.

Located at 277 Bancroft Road, London, E1 4DQ
Tel. 020 7364 1290
Website: www.ideastore.co.uk/local-history
Email address: localhistory@towerhamlets.gov.uk

The website should be visited prior to a physical visit in order to search the collections to see what there is that a researcher would wish to view. Photographs and maps can also be viewed there, and there is a short guide to genealogical sources available at THLHL&A, as well as a number of useful links for researchers of many aspects of East End history, and a brief bibliography of books relevant to East End family history.

Hackney Archives

Material relevant to Shoreditch history is held here as the borough was incorporated into the new London Borough of Hackney in 1965.

Opening hours: Tuesday and Wednesday, 10–6, Thursday, 10–7.30, Saturday 12.30–5. Closed on Sunday, Monday and Friday.

Located at Dalston Square, London E8 3BQ
Tel. 020 8356 8925
Website: www.hackney.gov.uk
Email address: archives@hackney.gov.uk

As with THLHL&A's website, photographs from the collection can be viewed online here. The catalogue to HA's collection can also be searched, too. This is not quite as straightforward as THLHL&A's, but is quite easy to navigate once the given instructions are followed. Instead of one general search engine, as with THLHL&A, there are two. One is the library catalogue, chiefly to printed, published material, such as leaflets, books and magazines. The catalogue to archives is via TNA's website. A link is provided here, and once TNA's site is located, it is necessary to click on 'Other Archives' and then type in the box 'Hackney Archives' in order to limit your search to archives to be found at HA.

Bring £8 for a photograph licence in order to photograph any items that you see there. It is necessary to search for the archives required on the online catalogue to order them in advance, but the maps, electoral registers, microfilmed newspapers and books are on open access

Guildhall Library

One of the three libraries operated by the Corporation of London (the local authority for the City of London), this is a reference library which contains a large collection of books on London's history as well as an unrivalled collection of directories. There is no need to make an appointment prior to visiting nor to possess a reader's ticket nor to provide proof of identity. The majority of books are on closed access. All you need to do is to search the library catalogues, complete a short form for each volume desired (six items can be ordered at any one time) and then wait for about 20 minutes depending on how busy the place is for the books to be delivered to your table. Whilst waiting you may wish to read some of the books on open access.

Located at Aldermanbury, London EC2P 2EJ
Tel. 020 7332 1868/1870
Website: www.cityoflondon.gov.uk
Email address: guildhall.library@city oflondon.gov.uk

Opening hours: Monday, Tuesday, Thursday and Friday, 9.30–5, Wednesday, 9.30–7.30, alternate Saturdays, 9.30–5. Closed on Sunday.

As with the other sites, you can search the library's catalogue prior to a visit, to save time when actually at the library.

Royal London Hospital Archives Centre and Museum

Holds the archives of a number of East End hospitals, listed in chapter 9. Located at 9 Prescot Street, London E1 8PR

Address for correspondence: Royal London Hospital Archives, Whitechapel Road, London E1 1BB

Tel. 020 7377 7608/020 7480 4823
Email address: rlharchives@bartshealth.nhs.uk
Website: www.barts/health.nhs.uk/about-us/museums-history-and-archives/the-royal-london-archives

Hackney Museum

Contains artefacts and other material relevant to the history of the London Borough of Hackney, so includes items relevant to Shoreditch's past. Some items can be seen online and can be searched therein. Regular programme of exhibitions and events.

1 Reading Lane, London E8 1GQ
Tel. 020 8356 3500
Email address: hmuseum@hackney.gov.uk
Website: https://www.hackney.gov.uk/museum

Opening hours: Tuesday, Wednesday and Friday, 9.30—5.30, Thursdays, 9.30–8, Saturday, 10–5

Museum of Immigration

Open by appointment for group visits only, this place charts the arrival of peoples in and out of London over the centuries. Appropriately it is housed in a building once used by the Huguenots.

19 Princelet Street, London E1 6QH
Tel. 020 7247 5352
Website: www.migrationmuseum.org

Museum of the Dockland

Part of the Museum of London, this museum tells the history of the River Thames and the docklands and the people who have worked there. It was opened in 2003 in this Grade I listed former warehouse. There are a dozen permanent galleries concerning topics such as trade, slavery, the docklands, Empire, sailors, the Second World War, and the decline and reinvention of the docklands at the end of the twentieth century.

No. 1 Warehouse, West Indies Quay, London E4 4AL
Tel. 020 7001 9844
Website: http://www.museumoflondon.org.uk/museum-london-docklands
Opening hours: 10-6, Monday to Saturday, free.

Jewish Museum

This museum charts the history of the Jews in England from the Middle Ages to the present, looking at family, faith and culture. Among the permanent exhibitions of particular relevance to this book is the reconstruction of part of the Jewish East End.

Raymond Burton House, 129–131 Albert Street, London NW1 7NB
Tel. 020 7284 7384
Website: www.jewishmuseum.org.uk
Email: admin@jewishmuseum.org.uk

Opening hours: 10–5, Monday to Thursday and Saturdays, 10–2 Fridays, £8.50 for adults.

Please note that opening hours and contact details of all these places were accurate at the time of writing (2017); they may have changed by the time that you are reading this, so please check before visiting.

The Modern East End

Walking in the footsteps of your ancestors has a strong appeal and is recommended, but great caution and care is also needed because the East End has changed immensely during the last century, in part because of the bombing during the Second World War, in part because of the slum clearance and rebuilding both before and after that conflict and finally because of the great changes brought about by immigration. But some buildings have survived and so help act as reminders for what our ancestors may have seen. Even then, buildings never remain in aspic and are being continually modified, especially internally, in order to meet the needs of the present and anticipate those of the future. For example, former industrial buildings may now be used as accommodation or office space, churches and schools will often have been radically redesigned for the needs of the present users. Many of the streets near Brick Lane, including this street itself, retain their Victorian exterior appearances.

One of the best guides to the contemporary East End buildings is the *Buildings of England, London 5: East*, by Bridget Cherry, Charles O'Brien and Nikolaus Pevsner (2005), since it gives concise accounts of existing buildings (at time of publication that is, but hopefully mostly still surviving now). The bulk of the book is a gazetteer divided between the six London boroughs, with Tower Hamlets covering pages 377–707. This is sub-divided into district, i.e. Spitalfields and Whitechapel, Mile End and Stepney Green, etc. Each of these sub-sections begins with a general introduction about building trends over the centuries, followed by a map, an examination of the extant religious buildings, then of major (secular) buildings such as hospitals, town halls, libraries, art galleries and so on, then a perambulation, which takes the reader on a guided tour around the streets, pointing out other buildings of note and merit. For Shoreditch, consult, in the same series, *London 4: North*, published in 1998 and written by Cherry and Pevsner. Shoreditch is included in the Hackney section and can be found on pages 512–31.

The reader will have to prioritise for themselves which buildings and streets they wish to see, and perhaps photograph. Needless to say, such expeditions are best undertaken on dry days which are not too sunny, armed with a map and a list of priorities. Essential sights will be determined by the researcher's previous research findings. Perhaps the obvious places to see might include the places where ancestors were born, baptised (if applicable), married and died, as well as where they were schooled and where they worked, as well as any other places known to have been associated with them. In some cases, imagination may be required, if applied logically and carefully and in the knowledge that this is reasonable supposition rather than known fact. For example, pubs near to where an ancestor lived and worked may well have been those that they patronised (assuming they still exist). Open House weekend in September is a free opportunity to enter buildings not usually open to the public, so is a good chance to do so; usually expert guides are on hand.

Walking Tours

It is also possible, for a fee, to go on a guided walking tour of the East End. One company, London Walks, at time of writing, runs several which are relevant for readers of this book. These are 'The Unknown East End', which looks at revolutionaries, restaurants and religion among other aspects of 'real people's London'. Then there is the 'Old Jewish Quarter', dealing with places of work and religion in Whitechapel and Spitalfields. These two run weekly. Running more often are the Jack the Ripper walks, of which there are several, run by such experts as Lindsay Sivitar. There are also occasional walks covering the East End of the Krays, Limehouse and the Docklands, and the East India Docks. These walks can show you aspects of the East End that you might not see otherwise and you could benefit from the knowledge of the guide.

There are also a number of walking tour leaflets that can be viewed on THLHL&A's website under 'Digital Resources'. These are as follows:

Gravestone of Henry Raine, brewer (photo taken by Paul Howard Lang, 2017).

Bengali Cultural Walk, Black History Walk, Jewish History Walk, Bow Heritage Trail, Spitalfields Walk, Wapping and Limehouse Walk and an Isle of Dogs Walk.

Virtual tours of the East End can be taken by visiting the East London History Society website. These are to London Hospital, Victoria Park, The People's Palace and a walk from Bromley to Bow along Mile End. These tours show exterior and interior pictures, maps and plans of the places in question, of varying dates. There is a tour which includes Shoreditch at http://walkhackney.co.uk.

Churches

Many churches have monumental inscriptions to former parishioners inside the buildings, on the walls and on the floors, mostly dating from the sixteenth to the nineteenth century. These contain information about the deceased, usually dates of birth and death, together with other family details and about their life. There may also be notes about their character, which will almost always be very praiseworthy. At St Dunstan's church in Stepney, the ancient parish church of the East End, are memorials to Sir Henry Colet who died in 1510 and was twice Lord Mayor of London, Robert Clarke who died a century later and his infant daughter, and Admiral Sir John Berry and Rebecca, his wife, who died in 1689 and 1696 respectively.

A memorial to more humble folk which exists in this church is as follows:

> Sacred to the memory of the following persons, who all suffered in one conflagration, on one day, and one hour, the third of June 1803.
> Mrs Barbara Ford, aged 71 years.
> Mr Joseph Williams, aged 42 years.
> Mary, his wife and daughter of the above
> Mrs Barbara Ford, aged 39 years
> Esther Williams, aged 13 years
> Joseph Williams, aged 9 years
> And Richard Williams, aged 7 years, children of the aforesaid Joseph and Mary Williams
> Tremulous God, thy sovereign power,
> Consum'd to atoms in one hour,
> Nor spar'd a father, mother, and a son
> Nor any to relate how it begun;
> Yet we must own that thou art just;
> That we are wretched sinful dust.

Churches with graveyards are also of interest, because of the tombstones and the information they may contain. Most people will not have gravestones, due to poverty, but many do. Some of these have been listed and so can be checked prior to a visit to the church. Many churches are routinely locked, so if you plan to visit contact the churchwardens or vicar in advance.

Churches often have boards listing former clergymen with dates of incumbencies, memorials for the fallen of the world wars (usually service personnel, with varying levels of details). They also have boards listing charities established by wealthy parishioners of the past. Unusually, St Leonard's Shoreditch has a stocks and whipping post. A number of these inscriptions have been published. For the East End these are:

> The Brasses of Middlesex, in *Transactions of the London and Middlesex Archaeological Society*, various articles, 1951–83
> Leslie Suggars and Christopher Watts, *St Anne's, Limehouse: Monumental Inscriptions*, Society of Genealogists, 1978
> Holy Trinity Mile End monumental inscriptions, microfiche by East London Family History Society, 1993
> P Whittemore, Monuments formerly in the church of St Leonard's Shoreditch, *Church Monuments*, 17 (2002)
> *The Church of St Dunstan, Stepney*, Monograph 6, Survey of the Memorials of Greater London, 1905

Cemeteries

Much information found about individuals will be in a two-dimensional format, but gravestones give an extra dimension, quite literally and so should be sought where possible. From the mid-nineteenth century the dead have been buried in cemeteries rather than the overcrowded churchyards. The main cemeteries in the East End are as follows.

Bethnal Green Jewish Cemetery, Brady Street

Established in 1795 by the Ashkenazi community – many late nineteenth-century tombs, including several Rothschild ones.

Jewish Cemetery, Mile End and Alderney Roads

The oldest Jewish cemetery in London, opened in 1657 and closed in 1758. Most of the tombstones lie flat.

Salmon Lane Nonconformist Cemetery

Established in 1779. Very small.

Tower Hamlets Cemetery, Southern Grove.

Established in 1841 as a private cemetery for St Dunstan's, Stepney, and St Leonard's, Bromley by Bow, this 33 acre site is rather overgrown and burials here ceased in 1966. Archives are held at the LMA: registers for consecrated ground, 1841–1966, registers for unconsecrated ground, 1841–1959, day books for both, 1841–1901, fee books, 1902–24 and 1944–66, private grave registers, 1841–1966 (indexed, 1841–1941) and registers for public graves (1900–1965). They provide the name of the deceased, their abode, age at death, by whom and when buried.

Victoria Park Cemetery

Opened in 1845 and closed in 1874 due to overcrowding.

Most cemeteries are open in daylight hours, but looking for an individual grave (assuming one exists), is a very time-consuming business unless you know the plot number. It is strongly advised to ascertain this prior to a visit as well as checking the cemetery opening hours.

War Memorials

The human cost of the world wars resulted in numerous war memorials being created. Some were located in churches, schools, workplaces as well as being created by public subscription; some names of the deceased may well appear on more than one. Not all memorials include names and some commemorate the sacrifices made in both wars. Those for what is now the London Borough of Tower Hamlets can be found on www.towerhamlets.gov.uk/Documents/Planning-and-building-control/conservation. There are 42 of these in all. A few are as follows:

1. On the south side of the recreation ground in Poplar to commemorate the 18 school children killed in bombing in 1917: on a plinth crowned with an angel.
2. In Grove Hall Park, Bow: a white stone cross.
3. On Bonner Street School, to commemorate men from Mace and Tagg streets killed in the First World War.

Websites

There are at least two websites which should be visited as well as those associated with the record offices, libraries and museums already mentioned.

The East of London Family History Society

https://eolfhs.org.uk: This society was founded in 1978 and covers the modern boroughs of Tower Hamlets, Newham, Hackney, Redbridge, Havering and Barking and Dagenham. There are two sections of the website. One is available to all and sundry, and this includes a copy of the society's publication, *Cockney Ancestor*, the street index for Stepney in 1871, surnames of interest to members and a number of information sheets, such as a programme of the society's events and a research guide. However, if you pay to become a member, you can see copies of the aforesaid journal, published quarterly, take part in the discussion groups, check other online resources and gain free entry to society meetings.

East London History Society

www.mernick.org.uk/elhs (email: mail@eastlondonhistory.org.uk): Founded in 1952 the group focuses on the history of Tower Hamlets, Newham and Hackney. Meetings are held at the Latimer Congregational Church hall, Ernest Street, London E1 4LS at 7.30 on the prescribed evenings. Their publication is the *East London Record*, three editions of which are published annually. Their website has a great many resources, picture galleries of photographs and postcards of the East End, old maps of East London, virtual tours of the London Hospital and Victoria Park using old maps, plans and photographs. There are links to other relevant groups such as the *East End Life* newspaper, Port of London Study Group, the London Trained Bands re-enactment group and much more. The site has a list of publications relevant to East London history.

Joining either or both groups is useful for it puts one in touch with like-minded enthusiasts. Historical research can be a lonely business if friends and family only have a limited interest in it. Attending meetings and taking part in online discussions can lead to additional sources of information previously untapped.

CONCLUSION

This book has attempted to scratch the surface of the vast amount of material available for the study if the East End and its residents. Hopefully it has indicated, not everything that exists, but a goodly proportion of what there is, scattered over a number of places, but heavily focused in a few.

By now it will be apparent that there are numerous sources for anyone interested in researching aspects of East End history and of those who lived there in the past. Not all will be relevant to all researchers, but some will certainly be crucial. The question now is, what next? For the family historian, the answer is perhaps easy to resolve, though it might be worth deciding which ancestor/s to focus on for trying to tackle all one's ancestors in one fell swoop would be an impossible task. The local historian needs to focus on what they want to do. It may be an East End wide topic, such as politics or industry, but even then, a time span might be necessary. Or it may be a study on a particular individual or group, a building or a set of them, or a particular part of the East End, or a particular period in history such as a decade or a war. Knowing what you want to achieve is vital before you can even start answering that question.

My suggestion is to try and read as much as you can before arriving at a record office or library or even the East End itself. This is of particular importance for the local historian. These articles and books should tell you what has already been written and what the questions posed are, the controversies and the answers provided by previous historians. Some of this research can, and indeed must, be carried out online. This is particularly the case for the family historian; Ancestry.co.uk is essential, in order to supply as much material as possible before a visit to undertake the research. All researchers into the East End should examine the websites of the LMA, HA and THLHL&A, in order to list what they want to see in advance of any visit, as time 'on the ground' as it were is limited. The websites of the East London History Society and the East London Family History Society should also be viewed, too.

It will probably take more than one visit to the East End in order to uncover all that can be found. Much depends on the extent and ambition of your project. Bear in mind that more material is being made available all the time, as archive offices receive new deposits and donations of archives and as closure periods lapse. The *East London Record* notes new acquisitions at THLHL&A and TNA's Discovery database will locate new material in record offices nationally. The East End does not stand still, nor do the sources for its history and research.

BIBLIOGRAPHY

There are countless books about London's history which contain useful information about the East End and its people, from John Stow and Daniel Lysons onwards. To include all would be impossible, so I am merely attempting below to list those especially relevant. This is, however, the tip of a very large iceberg: more titles can be found on the East London History website. Books already cited in the text are not listed here.

General

Walter Besant, *East London* (1901).

J G Birch, *Limehouse through Five Centuries* (1930).

Jane Cox, *London's East End: Life and Traditions* (1994).

Henry Ellis, *History and Antiquities of the Parish of St. Leonard's Shoreditch and Norton Folgate*, 3 volumes (1845).

Brian Girling, *East End Neighbourhoods* (2005).

Guide to Greater London History Sources, vols 1 (The City) and 2 (Middlesex) (2004, 2006).

Gary Haines, *Images of London: Bethnal Green* (2002).

Colin Kerrigan, *A History of Tower Hamlets* (1982).

Steve Lewis, *London's East End: Then and Now* (n.d.)

David Mander, *More Light, More Power: An Illustrated History of Shoreditch* (1996).

John Marriott, *Beyond the Tower: A History of East London* (2011).

Alan Palmer, *The East End* (1989).

Tony Phillips, *London Docklands Guide* (1986).

Robert Phillpots, *One Foot in the East End* (1992).

Millicent Rose, *The East End of London* (1973).

Sir Herbert Llewellyn Smith, *The History of East London from the Earliest Times to the Eighteenth Century* (1939).

Richard Tames, *East End Past* (2002).

Rosemary Taylor and Christopher Lloyd, *A Century of the East End* (1999).

Transactions of the London and Middlesex Archaeological Society, 1860–

Victoria County History of Middlesex (volumes 1 and 2 cover the county generally; volume 11 covers Stepney and Poplar). Can be accessed on www.british-history.ac.uk

Michael Young and Peter Wilmott, *Family and Kinship in East London* (1957).

Buildings

Bridget Cherry, C. O'Brien, Nikolaus Pevsner, *The Buildings of England: London 5: East* (2005).

Bridget Cherry and Nikolaus Pevsner, *The Buildings of England: London 4: North* (1998).

The Survey of London, vol. 7, Shoreditch (1922).

The Survey of London, vol. 27, *Spitalfields and Mile End New Town* (1957).

Memoirs

Robert Barltrop and Jim Wolveridge, *The Muvver Tongue* (1980).

Anita Dobson, *My Eastend* (1987).

Grace Foakes, *My Part of the River* (1974).

Emmanuel Litvinoff, *Journey through a Small Planet* (1993).

Arthur Ernest Newens, *The Memoirs of an Old East Ender* (2001).

Dorothy Scannell, *Mother Knew Best* (1974).

Ben Thomas, *Ben's Limehouse* (1987).

Simon Webb, *A 1960s East End Childhood* (2012).

Jennifer Worth, *In the Shadows of the Workhouse* (2005).

Genealogical

Kathy Chater, *Tracing Your Huguenot Ancestors* (2012).

Jane Cox, *Tracing Your East End Ancestors* (2011).

Jonathan Oates, *Tracing Your London Ancestors* (2011).

Jonathan Oates, *Tracing Villains and their Victims* (2017).

R Swift, *Irish Immigrants in Britain, 1815–1914* (2002).

Rachel Wenzerul, *Tracing Your Jewish Ancestors* (2008).

Poor Law

Phillip Davis, *The Bromley Workhouse of the Stepney Union, 1863–1900: A Case Study* (1997).

George Lanbury, *The Development of the Human Administration of the Poor Law under the Poplar Board of Health* (c.1907).

Juliana May, *The Administration of the Poor Law in Poplar from the Late Sixteenth Century to the Early Nineteenth Century* (1967).

Ellen Ross, *Slum Travellers: Ladies and London Poverty, 1860–1920* (2007).

Pat Ryan, *Politics and Relief: East London Unions in the Later Nineteenth and Early Twentieth Centuries* (1985).

War and Disaster

Tony Butler, ed., *The 1943 Bethnal Green Tube Shelter Disaster* (2015).

Eve Hosteller, ed., *The Island at War: Memories of Wartime Life on the Isle of Dogs* (1985).

Christopher Lloyd, *Tower Hamlets at War* (1985).

Christopher Lloyd and Rosemary Taylor, *The East End at War* (2000).

Ron Wilcox, *The Poplars* [local regiment raised in First World War] (2005).

Moving In

Yousuf Chudhury, *Sons of Empire: Oral History from the Bangladeshi Seamen Who Served British Ships during World War Two* (1995).

John Eade, ed., *Tales of Three Generations of Bengalis* (2006).

William Fishman, *East End Jewish Radicals, 1875–1914* (1975).

Kathy Gardner, *Narrating Location: Space, Age and Gender among Bengali Elders in East London* (1999).

William Goldsmith, *East End: My Cradle* (1947).

Rose Henriques, *Fifty Years in Stepney* (1966).

Benjamin Lanmers, *A Superior Kind of England: Jewish Ethnicity and English in London's East End, 1905–1939* (1997).

A B Levy, *East End Story: Observations, Anecdotes and Reminiscences* (1954).

Lawrence Rigal, *The Settlement Synagogue: Story of a Synagogue, 1919–1996* (1999).

Various authors, *The Jewish East End, 1850–1939* (1981).

Jerry White, *Rothschild Buildings: Life in an East End Tenement Block, 1887–1920* (1980).

Leisure

Hilary Hefferman, *The Annual Hop; London to Kent* (1996).

Gavin McGarth, *Cinemas and Theatres of Tower Hamlets* (2010).

Philip Mernick, *A Picture History of Victoria Park* (1996).

Gilda O'Neill, *Roll No More Bines: An Oral History of East London Women Hop Pickers* (1990).